W9-ARW-794

300 WONDERFUL FACTS TO CELEBRATE THE MAGIC OF DISNEY

NATIONAL GEOGRAPHIC
WASHINGTON, D.C.

EEPER
EPER

When ride vehicles from **Dumbo the Flying Elephant and the Mad Tea Party** were donated to the Smithsonian Institution, they received a **police escort** through **Washington, D.C.**

SPACESHIP EARTH
at EPCOT weighs about 16 million pounds (7 million kg).
The fastest ride at the Walt Disney World Resort is
Test Track at EPCOT–
the cars go almost
65 miles an hour (104 km/h).

On SPACE MOUNTAIN at the Magic Kingdom, a spaceship's signage reads H-NCH 1975, which refers to the last name of the ride's designer (Hench) and the year the ride opened.

Walt Disney had an apartment above the Town Square Fire Station at Disneyland.
To honor Walt Disney today, a lamp in the window is always lit.

105
DISNEYLAND
FIRE DEPT.
105

The actor who voiced
Donald Duck
also voiced the dog barks for One Hundred and One Dalmatians (1961).
Cucumbers in The Land pavilion greenhouses at EPCOT are grown in the shape of Mickey Mouse's head.
The water in the Jungle Cruise attraction is dyed.

THIRTEEN LANTERNS
hang from the Liberty Tree in
Liberty Square
at the Magic Kingdom—each represents one of
America's original
13 Colonies.

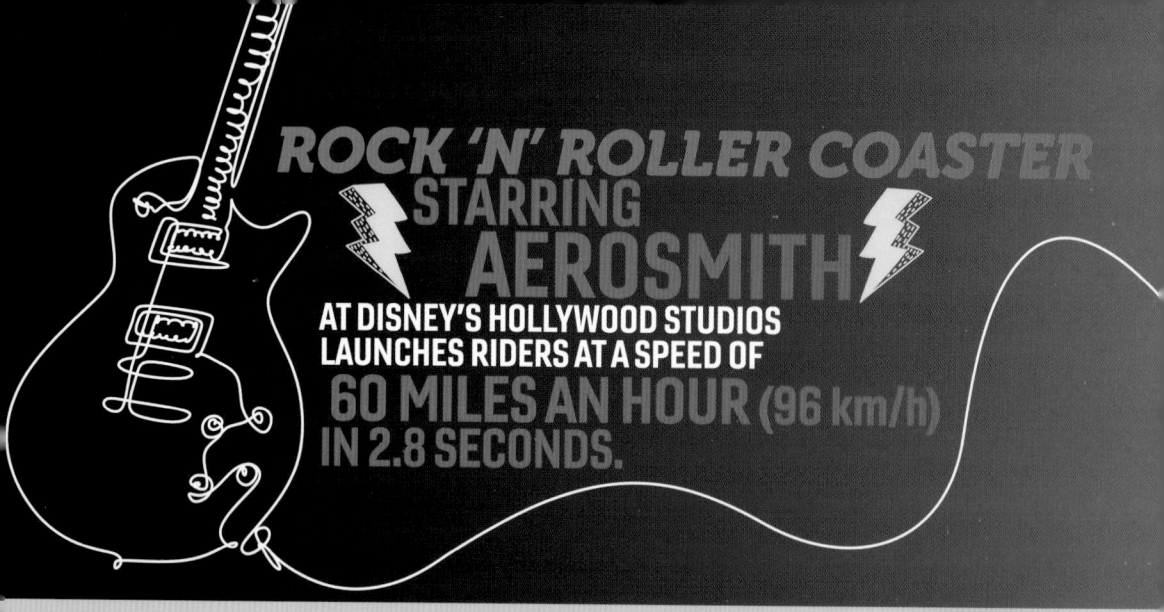

Animators studied the **movement of Rapunzel's hair** in *Tangled* (2010) to create the **movement of the ocean** in *Moana* (2016).

Tuk Tuk's design in *Raya and the Last Dragon* (2021) is inspired by a combination of a **roly-poly and a pug.**

THE REPLICA OF THE **LIBERTY BELL** IN LIBERTY SQUARE AT THE MAGIC KINGDOM WAS BUILT FROM THE **SAME CAST AS THE ORIGINAL.**

That's weird!

THE
ANIMAL
CARE
TEAM
AT DISNEY'S
ANIMAL KINGDOM
PREPARES
MORE THAN
4.5 TONS
(4 T)
OF FOOD
A DAY.

WALT DISNEY
was the voice of
MICKEY MOUSE
for almost 20 years.

The director of *Lightyear* (2022) built LEGO® models to share ideas for BUZZ'S SPACESHIP with fellow filmmakers.

One dress worn in *Descendants 2* (2017) took more than 100 yards (91 m) of fabric to make—that's almost the height of the Statue of Liberty.

A MAGIC TRICK from the 1800s makes dancing ghosts appear in the ballroom of the Haunted Mansion attraction.

The animated dogs in *One Hundred and One Dalmatians* (1961) sport a total of 6,469,952 spots.

Dino-Sue at Disney's Animal Kingdom is a reproduction of the most complete Tyrannosaurus rex skeleton ever discovered.
That's weird!

THE ARTISTS WHO DESIGN AND CREATE EACH DETAIL OF DISNEY THEME PARKS ARE CALLED IMAGINEERS—A COMBINATION OF "IMAGINATION" AND "ENGINEER."

A sign on Test Track at EPCOT shows the number 82, which references the year the theme park opened.

CRATERS ON THE PLANET MERCURY FORM THE SHAPE OF MICKEY MOUSE'S HEAD.

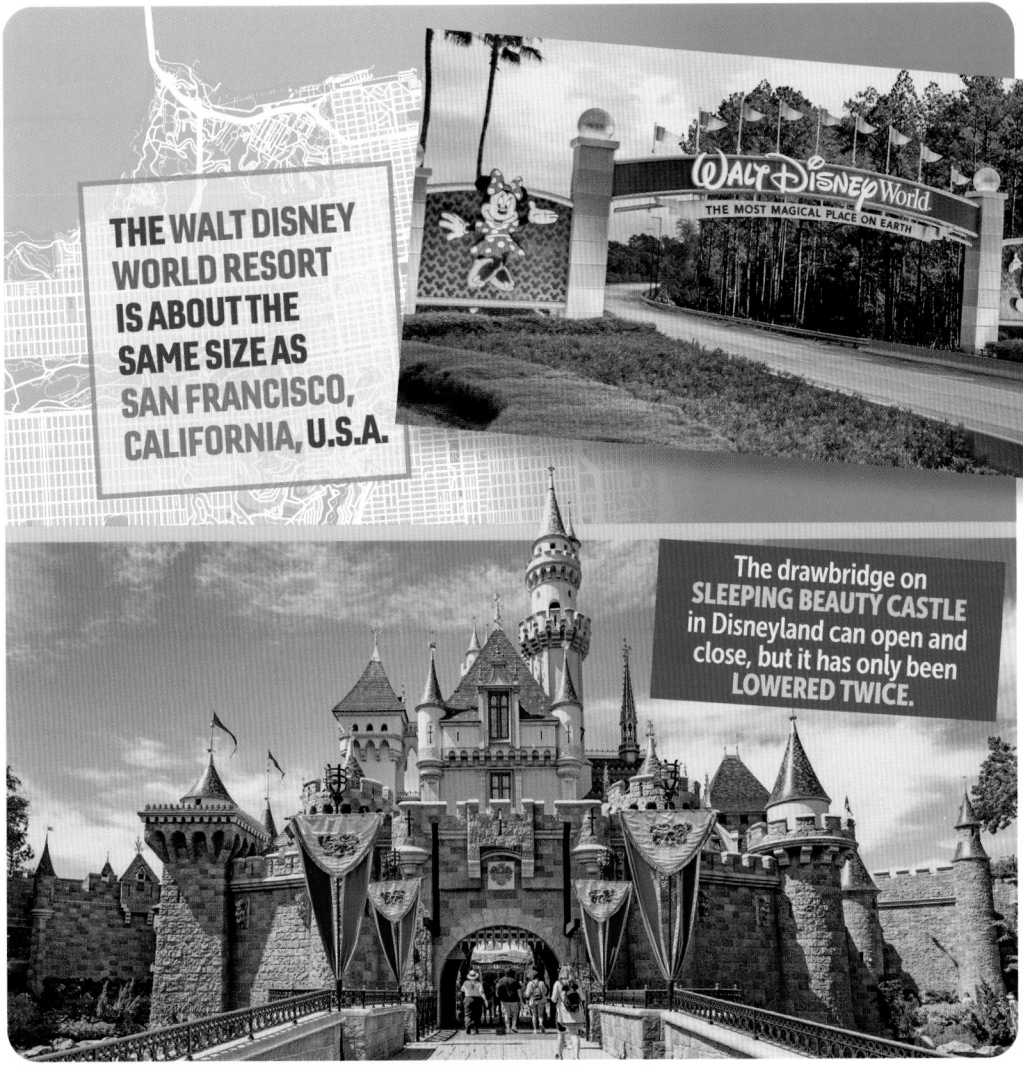

THE WALT DISNEY WORLD RESORT IS ABOUT THE SAME SIZE AS SAN FRANCISCO, CALIFORNIA, U.S.A.

The drawbridge on SLEEPING BEAUTY CASTLE in Disneyland can open and close, but it has only been LOWERED TWICE.

Filming STOPPED on Swiss Family Robinson (1960) when 100 FLAMINGO "STARS" suddenly migrated SOUTH.
The first words Mickey Mouse spoke were "Hot dog!" in a 1929 cartoon.
The NAMES ON THE TOMBSTONES outside the Haunted Mansion in the Magic Kingdom and Disneyland represent the Imagineers who created the attraction.

THE SORCERER IN *FANTASIA* (1940) IS NAMED YEN SID, WHICH IS "DISNEY" SPELLED BACKWARD.

Hidden Mickeys—often shown as one big circle for Mickey's head and two smaller ones for his ears—

can be found all over Disney properties.

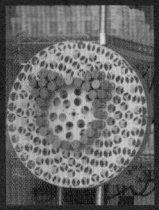

TWO SOLAR FACILITIES AT WALT DISNEY WORLD RESORT PROVIDE ENOUGH RENEWABLE ENERGY ANNUALLY TO OPERATE TWO OF THE RESORT'S FOUR THEME PARKS.

ONE FACILITY IS IN THE SHAPE OF MICKEY MOUSE'S HEAD.

Animators HANDCRAFTED hundreds of thousands of BUBBLES for *The Little Mermaid* (1989).

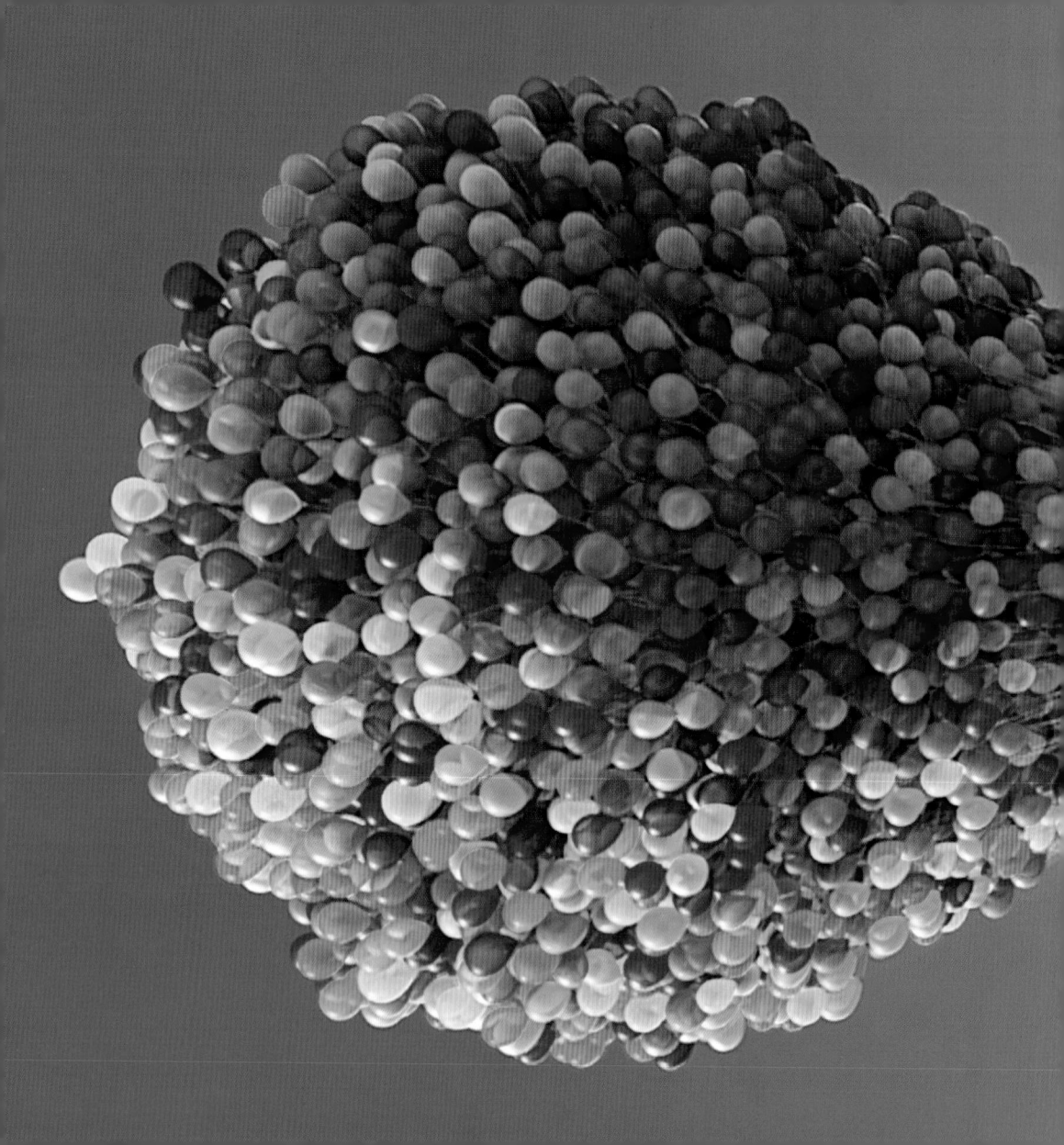

In *Up* (2009), **20,622 balloons** lifted Carl's house, but it would take more than **20 million balloons** to carry it in real life.

Walt Disney originally wanted to name Mickey Mouse "MORTIMER."
Toy blocks in the nursery in Peter Pan's Flight in Disneyland spell "Peter Pan."
A special machine blasts specific scents in different park attractions, such as salty sea air in Pirates of the Caribbean.

ON THE **SOARIN' AROUND THE WORLD** attraction, specific scents are released during certain scenes, such as the **SMELL OF GRASS AS YOU FLY OVER AFRICA.**

It took animators MORE THAN TWO YEARS to create the two-and-a-half-minute wildebeest stampede in *The Lion King* (1994).

Dumbo is the only title character from a Disney animated feature film who never speaks.

WHEN ALADDIN LIES TO JASMINE ABOUT BEING A PRINCE, THE FEATHER ON HIS HAT FALLS IN HIS FACE.
Snow White is the only Disney Princess with a star on the Hollywood Walk of Fame.
SNOW WHITE
Rapunzel's hair in *Tangled* (2010) has about 140,000 strands.

INK

Walt Disney's **first named animated character** was **Julius the cat.**

SCIENTISTS FROM DISNEY'S ANIMAL KINGDOM DISCOVERED THAT **elephants make a specific call** to warn their herd that **bees are nearby.**

looked like 2,000 years ago for Moana (2016).

Artists used more than **800 gallons** (3,028 L) of paint to animate *One Hundred and One Dalmatians* (1961)—that's enough to cover about **15 football fields.**

A SERIES OF TUNNELS CALLED THE UTILIDOR WAS BUILT UNDERNEATH THE MAGIC KINGDOM AT WALT DISNEY WORLD.

CAST MEMBERS USE THESE TUNNELS TO GET TO THEIR WORK LOCATIONS—WALT DISNEY WANTED IT TO SEEM AS IF THEY APPEAR BY MAGIC.

Goofy's
original
name was
Dippy
Dawg.

A PIZZERIA IN THE ITALY PAVILION AT EPCOT HAS THREE PIZZA OVENS THAT ARE NAMED AFTER ITALY'S THREE ACTIVE VOLCANOES:

ETNA, VESUVIUS, AND STROMBOLI.

Part of the live-action *Mulan* (2020) was filmed in China's Mingsha Mountains, which make a musical sound when the wind blows across them.

Main Street, U.S.A. in Disneyland draws inspiration from Walt Disney's hometown of Marceline, Missouri.

A restaurant in
Cinderella Castle
in the Magic Kingdom once offered diners medieval costumes to wear.
THE
WALT DISNEY WORLD RAILROAD
IN THE MAGIC KINGDOM OPERATES FOUR STEAM-POWERED TRAINS, SOME OF WHICH ARE
MORE THAN 100 YEARS OLD.

On
Main Street, U.S.A.
at Disney parks,
names of people who were important
to each park appear on the windows.
ORANGE GROVE
TEA
There's a basketball hoop inside the Matterhorn mountain in Disneyland.

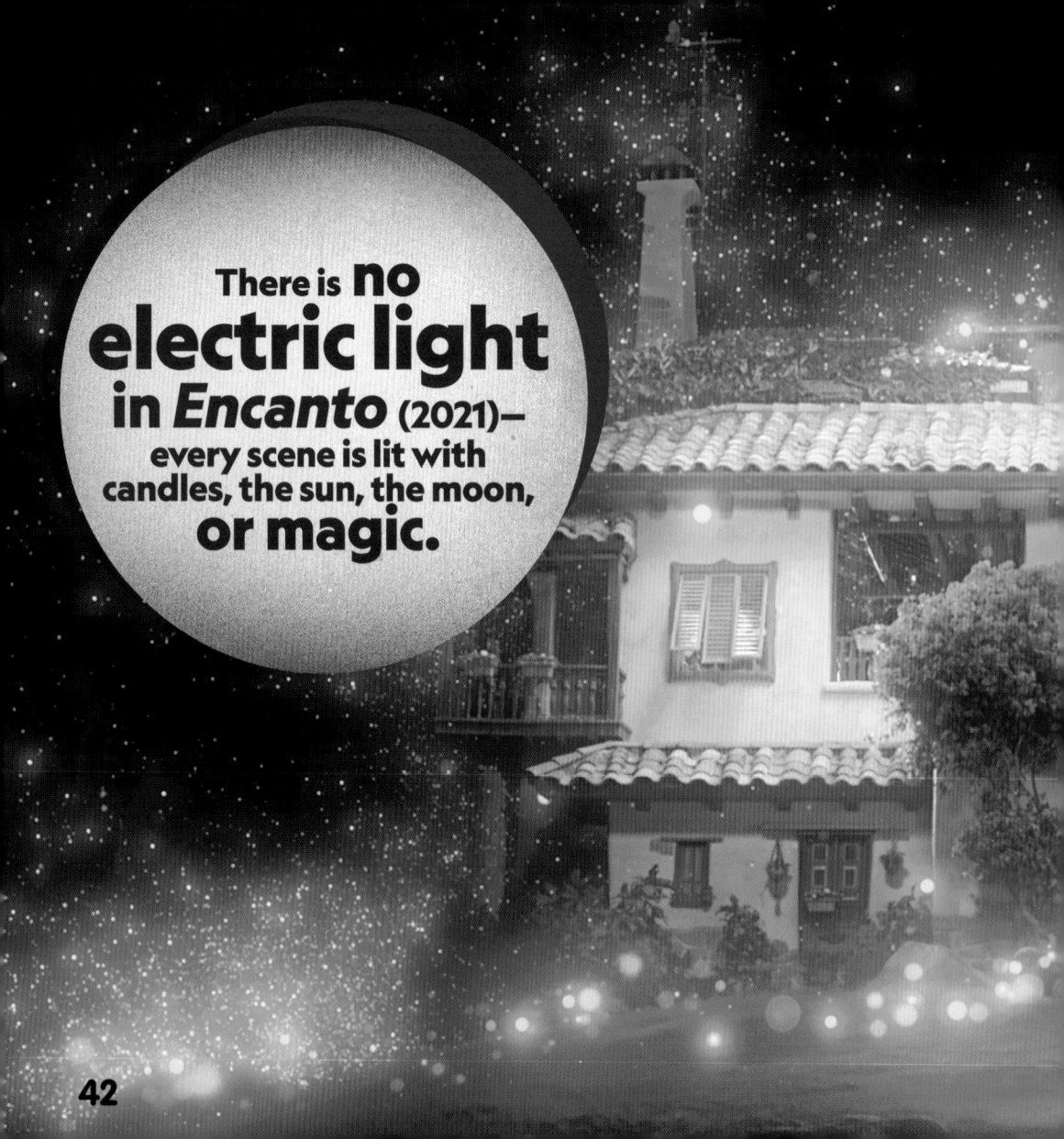

There is **no electric light** in ***Encanto*** (2021)— every scene is lit with candles, the sun, the moon, **or magic.**

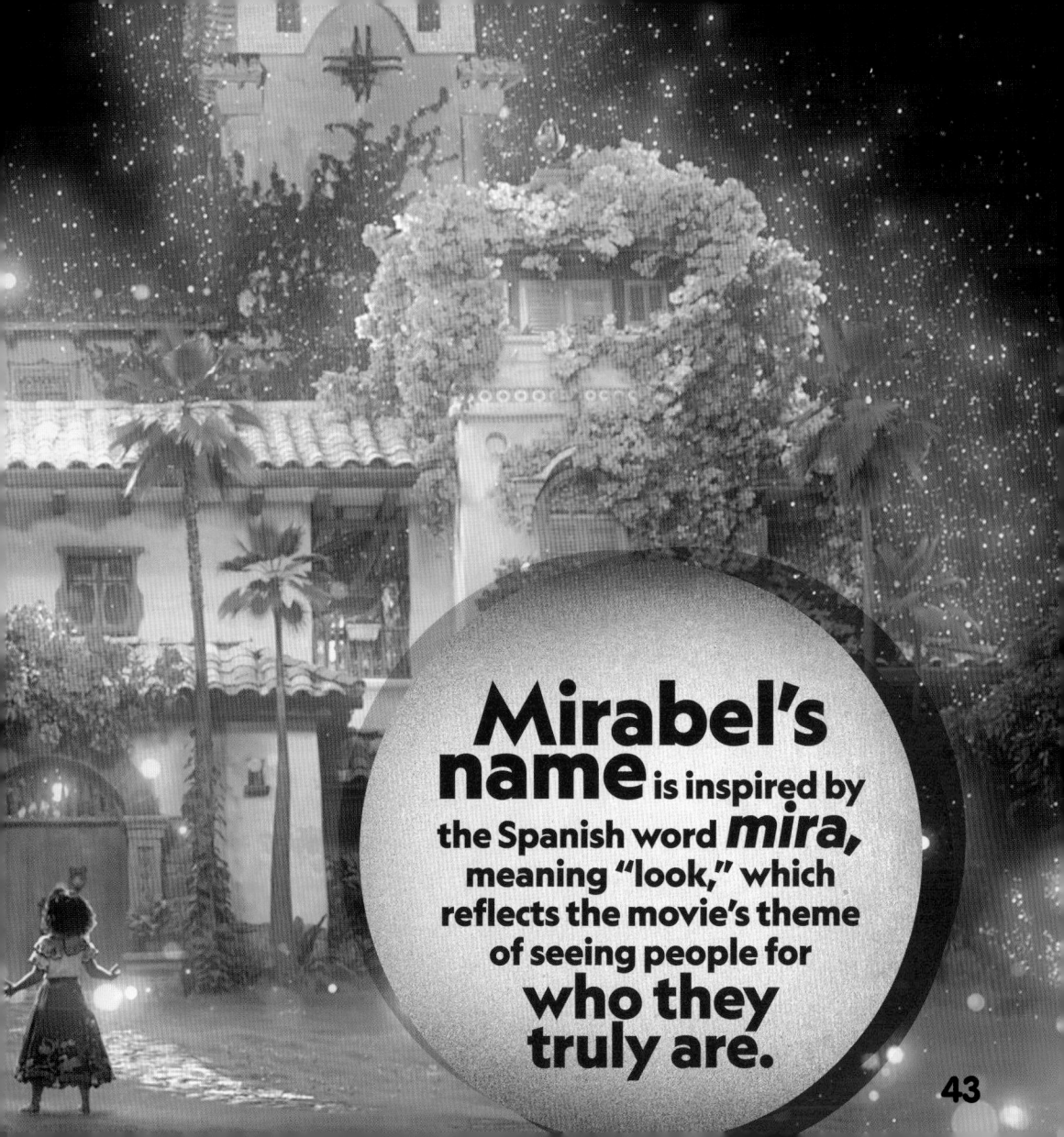

Mirabel's name is inspired by the Spanish word ***mira,*** meaning "look," which reflects the movie's theme of seeing people for **who they truly are.**

There's a suite inside Cinderella Castle in the Magic Kingdom.

On the KILIMANJARO SAFARIS savanna at Disney's Animal Kingdom, air is piped into rocks to **cool the cats.**

MORE THAN **4,000 PAIRS OF EARS** were sculpted for the LEPrecon characters in *Artemis Fowl* (2020).

AT DISNEY'S ANIMAL KINGDOM, THE TREE OF LIFE HAS MORE THAN 300 ANIMAL IMAGES CARVED INTO ITS TRUNK AND ROOTS.

The animated Beast in *Beauty and the Beast* (1991) is inspired by a mix of a lion, a buffalo, a wild boar, a gorilla, a wolf, and a bear.

Vegetables grown in The Land pavilion at **EPCOT** are used in some of the park's restaurants.

When rain falls on Spaceship Earth at EPCOT, the water is funneled through the sphere and into the park's World Showcase Lagoon.
The 29 GOLD SPHERES on the moon model in Mission: Space at Planetary Plaza at EPCOT represent the 29 U.S. and Soviet Union lunar landing missions between 1959 and 1976.

***Finding Nemo* (2003) artists went scuba diving to ensure the animated characters' accuracy.**

It took **28 people to operate** the remote controls that moved the mechanical **giant squid** in *20,000 Leagues Under the Sea* (1954).

The rooms in Disney's Contemporary Resort, near the Magic Kingdom, were built elsewhere, and then cranes slid them into the building's framework.

Donald Duck's middle name is Fauntleroy.
PEANUTS

TO CELEBRATE ITS

25th ANNIVERSARY,

THE WALT DISNEY WORLD RESORT TRANSFORMED

Cinderella Castle

INTO A CAKE, USING

400 gallons (1,514 L)

OF **PINK** PAINT.

It was topped with candles as high as 40 feet (12 m), 30 three-foot (0.9-m)-wide **lollipops,** and four 25-foot (7.6-m) stacks of **ring-shaped candies.**

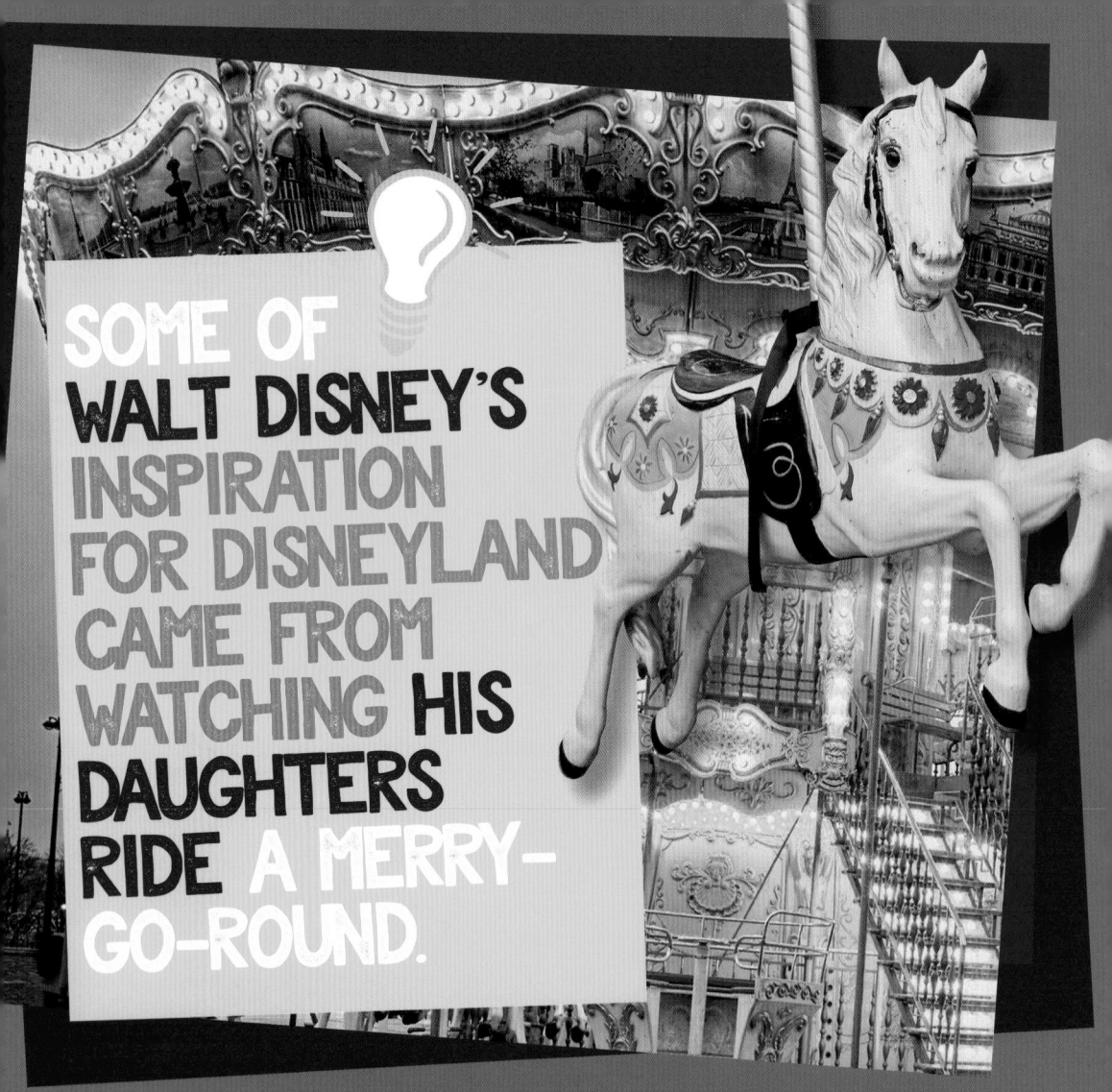

SOME OF WALT DISNEY'S INSPIRATION FOR DISNEYLAND CAME FROM WATCHING HIS DAUGHTERS RIDE A MERRY-GO-ROUND.

In the line for Slinky Dog Dash in Toy Story Land at Disney's Hollywood Studios, a Rex toy box shows a **$19.95 price tag,** which refers to the year that *Toy Story* opened in theaters.

One of Walt Disney's inspirations for **Sleeping Beauty Castle** in Disneyland was Neuschwanstein Castle in Germany.

Helicopters were used to shoot the footage for Soarin' Around the World.

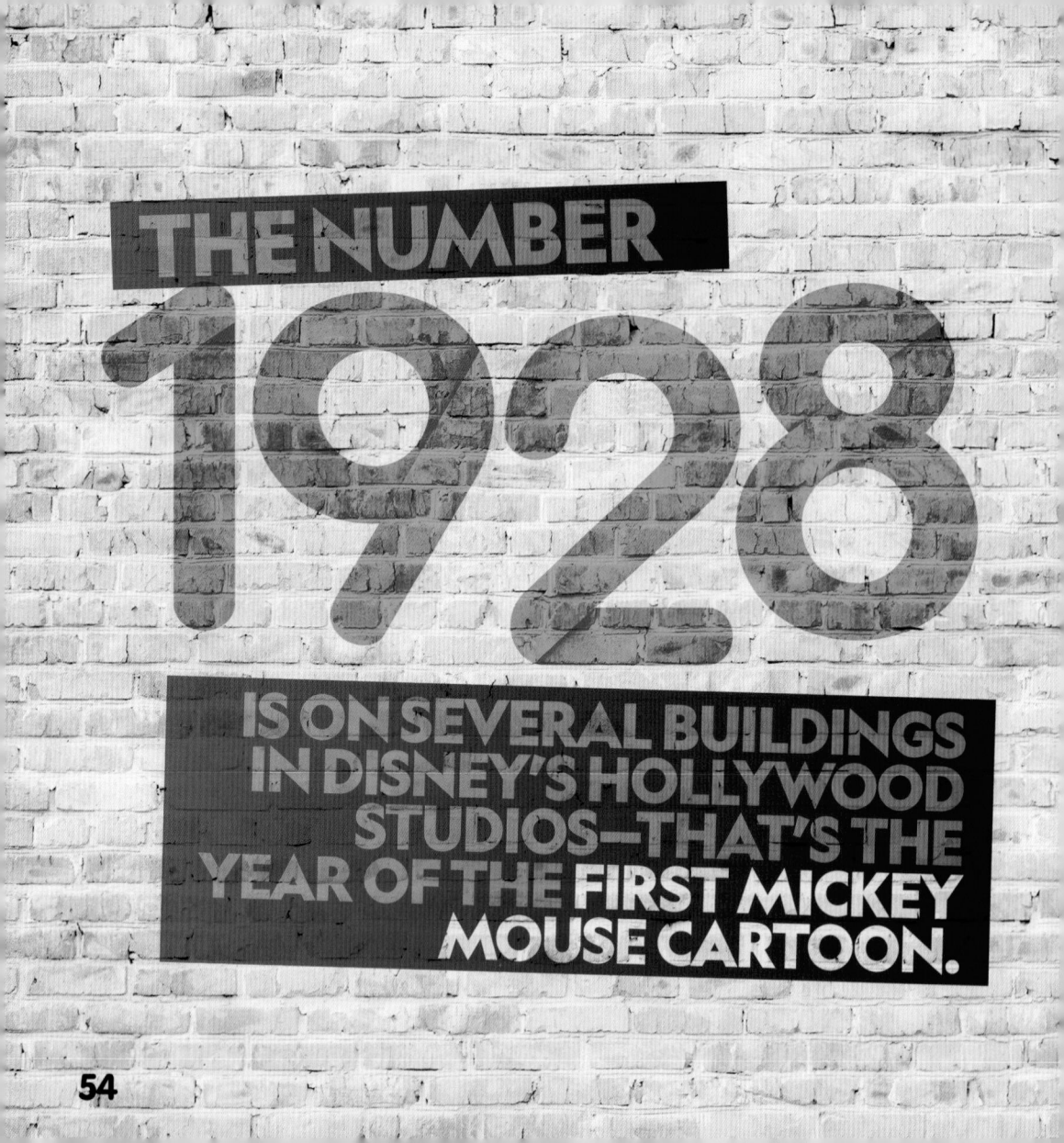
THE NUMBER
1928
IS ON SEVERAL BUILDINGS IN DISNEY'S HOLLYWOOD STUDIOS—THAT'S THE YEAR OF THE FIRST MICKEY MOUSE CARTOON.

A floral sculpture of Mickey Mouse in Dubai Miracle Garden, in the UNITED ARAB EMIRATES, is about as tall as a SIX-STORY BUILDING.

The **AQUADUCK** on the *Disney Dream* cruise ship was the first water coaster at sea.

Riders tube over the edge of the ship and back, **SWOOSHING** past four decks.

A chimpanzee carving on the **Tree of Life** at Disney's Animal Kingdom is of **David Greybeard,** the first chimp observed **using a tool** in the wild.

Primatologist **Jane Goodall** named him, and his is the **only carving** on the tree that's modeled after an individual animal.

THE SLINKY DOG DASH COASTER at Disney's Hollywood Studios **stops during the ride** and then sends you over a hill, a design crafted to imitate a **pull-back-and-launch toy.**

The **Dumbo octopus** is named for the large, earlike fins that it uses to move through the water.

FOR THE OPENING SCENE IN THE LAND OF THE DEAD IN *COCO* (2017), ANIMATORS CREATED **8.5 MILLION LIGHTS.**

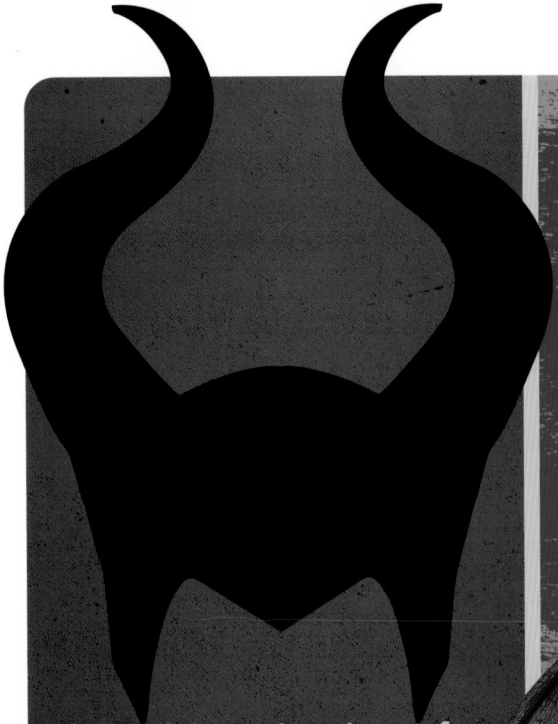

To celebrate the release of *Maleficent* (2014), a world-record number of people dressed as princesses gathered outside a theater in England.

COREY THE MANTICORE IN *ONWARD* (2020) IS A COMBINATION OF A LION, A SCORPION, A BAT, AND A HUMAN.

Artists carved concrete using crumpled aluminum foil to create the craggy look of the Himalaya mountains at Disney's Animal Kingdom.

In 2018, one woman set a world record by visiting all 12 Disney theme parks, and going on at least one attraction in each, in 75 hours 6 minutes.

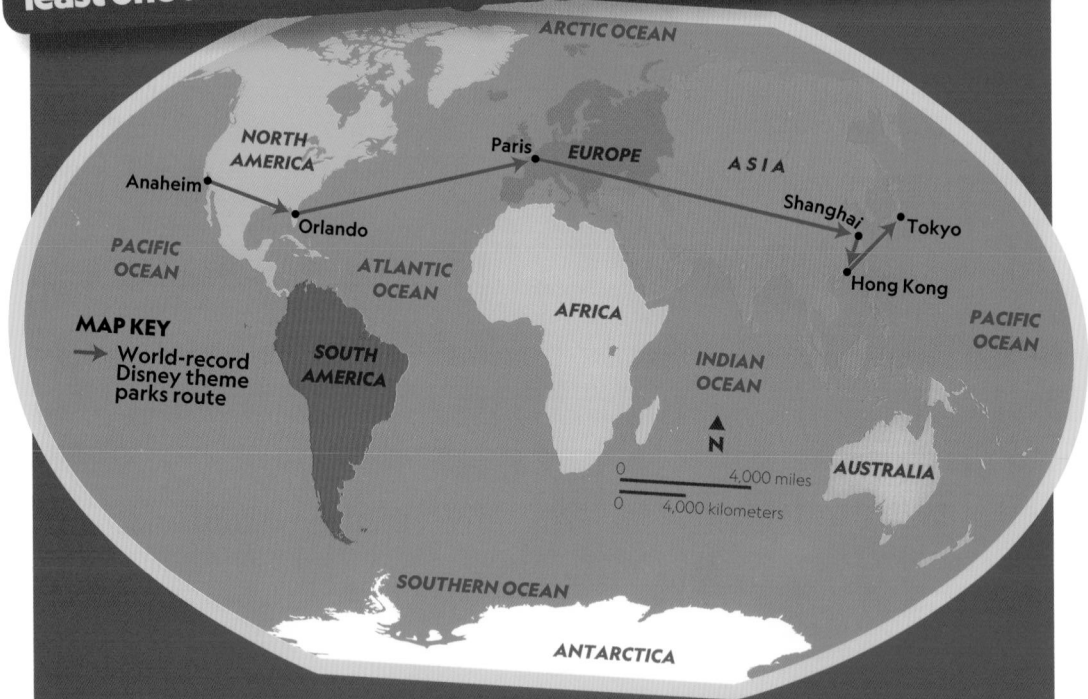

To celebrate Disneyland's **50th anniversary** in 2005, vehicles from opening-day attractions were painted **gold.**

BUZZ LIGHTYEAR from *Toy Story* (1995) was named for astronaut **BUZZ ALDRIN,** who was one of the first two people to walk on the moon.

To illustrate how Anton Ego, the **HARSH FOOD CRITIC** in *Ratatouille* (2007), **STRIKES FEAR INTO CHEFS,** his office is shaped like a coffin, and his **TYPEWRITER LIKE A SKULL.**

Bill Clinton
was the first
U.S. president
to provide his
voice for his
Audio-
Animatronics®
figure in the
Hall of Presidents
at the Magic
Kingdom.

To celebrate Goofy's

90th birthday

in 2022, one woman set a record for collecting the largest number of Goofy memorabilia—

1,825 items.

Walt Disney's teacher asked his class to draw flowers; Disney's had human faces and arms with hands.

THE **TELEGRAPH CODE** HEARD AT THE DISNEYLAND RAILROAD'S NEW ORLEANS SQUARE STATION **SPELLS OUT** WALT DISNEY'S SPEECH ON THE PARK'S **OPENING DAY, JULY 17, 1955.**

It takes **1,440 separate sketches** to create **one minute** of hand-drawn animation.

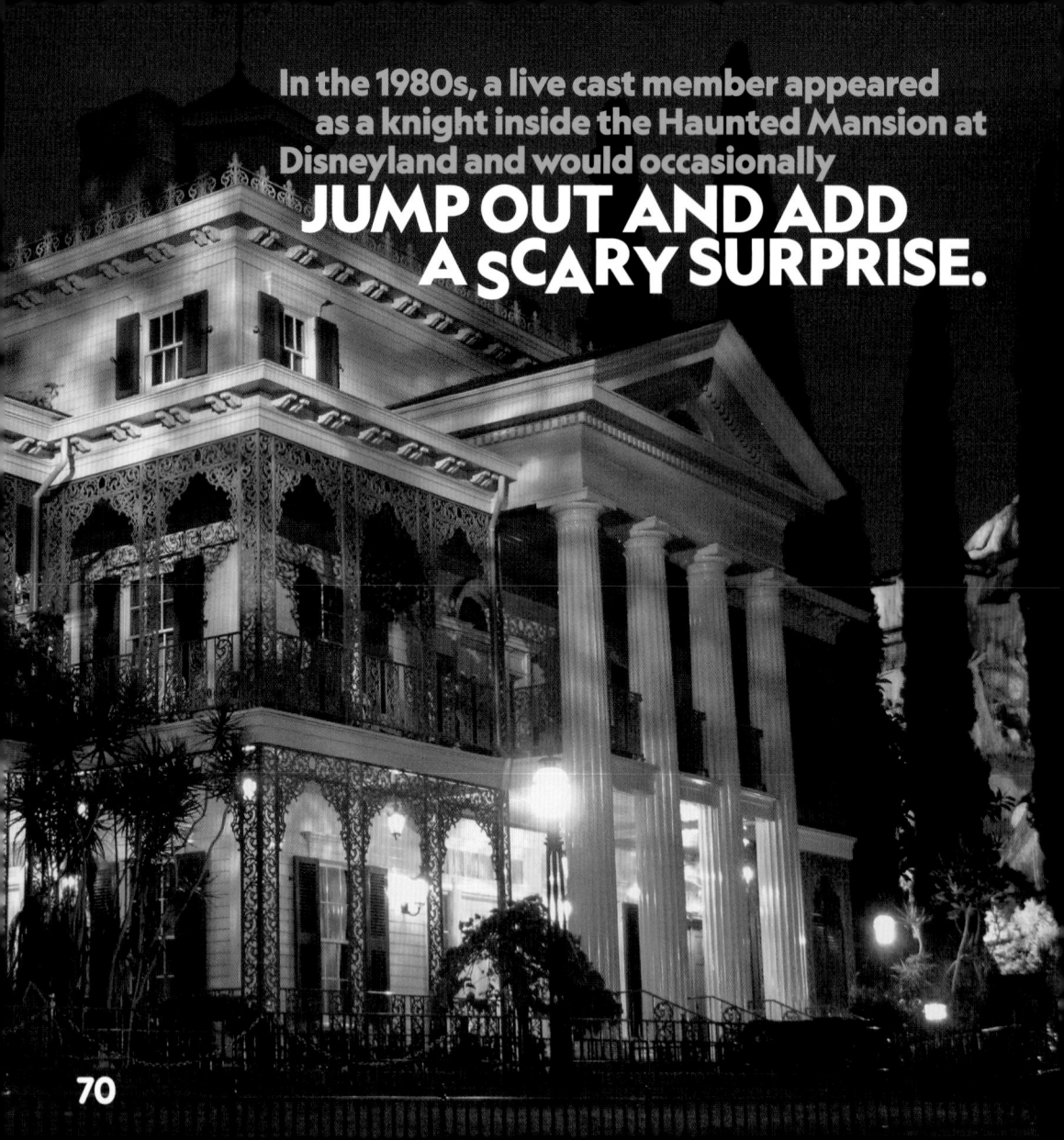

In the 1980s, a live cast member appeared as a knight inside the Haunted Mansion at Disneyland and would occasionally **JUMP OUT AND ADD A SCARY SURPRISE.**

There are **13** candles on the birthday cake in the ballroom at the **Haunted Mansion.**

Toy Story (1995) animators studied the movements of the Scarecrow in *The Wizard of Oz* (1939) as an example of how a stuffed character, like Woody, could
flop
and
bend.

THE CHRISTMAS TREE DISPLAYED IN TOWN SQUARE AT THE MAGIC KINGDOM **WEIGHS 16.5 TONS** (15 T) AND IS STRUNG WITH **5,400 LIGHTS.**

The **Pumpkin Trees** on each of the **Disney Cruise Line ships,** which only **"blossom"** during the Halloween season, are named **Grim, Mucklebones, Bog, Reap, and Boo.**

THE **OLDEST OBJECT** AT DISNEYLAND IS A **75-MILLION-YEAR-OLD PETRIFIED TREE.**

FOR A **Halloween celebration** AT DISNEYLAND IN 1995, CAST MEMBERS CARVED A PUMPKIN THAT WEIGHED 516 POUNDS (234 KG)—ABOUT AS MUCH AS A SIBERIAN TIGER.

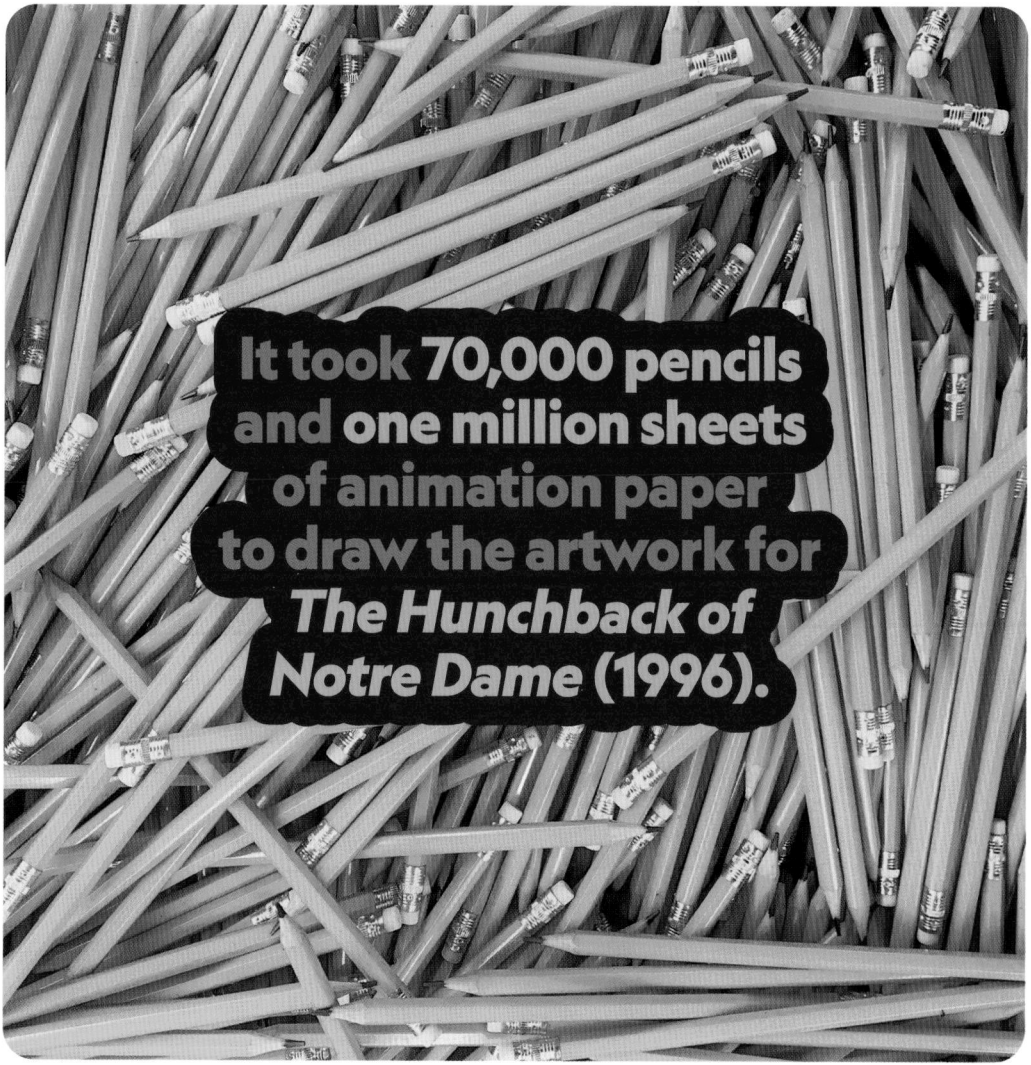
It took 70,000 pencils
and one million sheets
of animation paper
to draw the artwork for
The Hunchback of
Notre Dame (1996).

UP (2009)

ANIMATORS traveled to SOUTH AMERICA to research the alien-like *tepuis*, MILE-HIGH (0.6-km) TABLETOP MOUNTAINS in the rainforest.

To understand how the **Green Army Soldiers** would move in the Toy Story movies, animators **stuck shoes on a board** and then walked in them.

Walt Disney would often **stand in line** with his guests at Disneyland while they **waited to board a ride.**

The LIGHTHOUSE built for *Pete's Dragon* (1977) was so authentic that the film crew had to get PERMISSION FROM THE UNITED STATES COAST GUARD to use it.
Goat horns were the inspiration for Maleficent's headdress in ***Sleeping Beauty*** (1959).

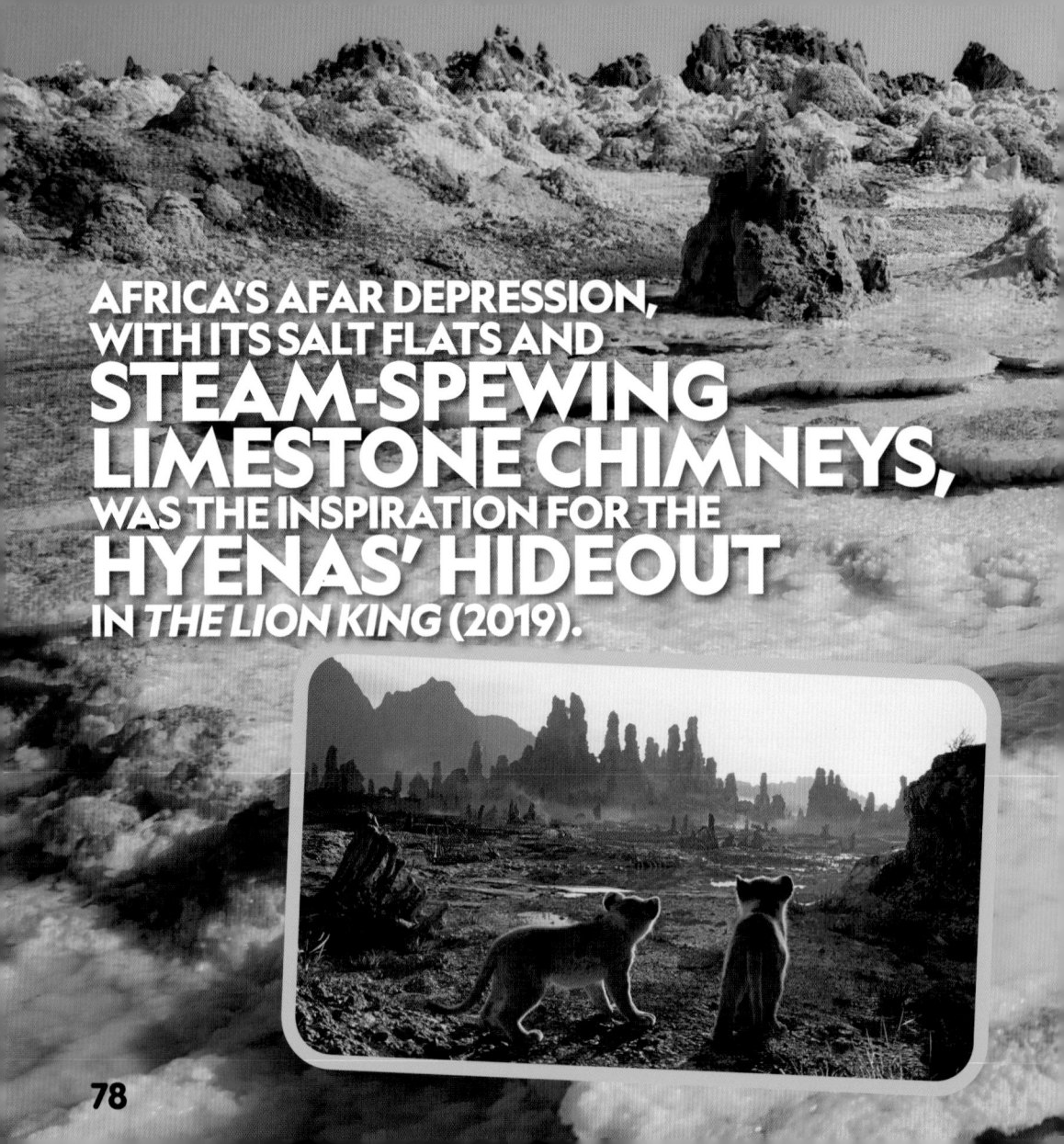

AFRICA'S AFAR DEPRESSION, WITH ITS SALT FLATS AND **STEAM-SPEWING LIMESTONE CHIMNEYS,** WAS THE INSPIRATION FOR THE **HYENAS' HIDEOUT** IN *THE LION KING* (2019).

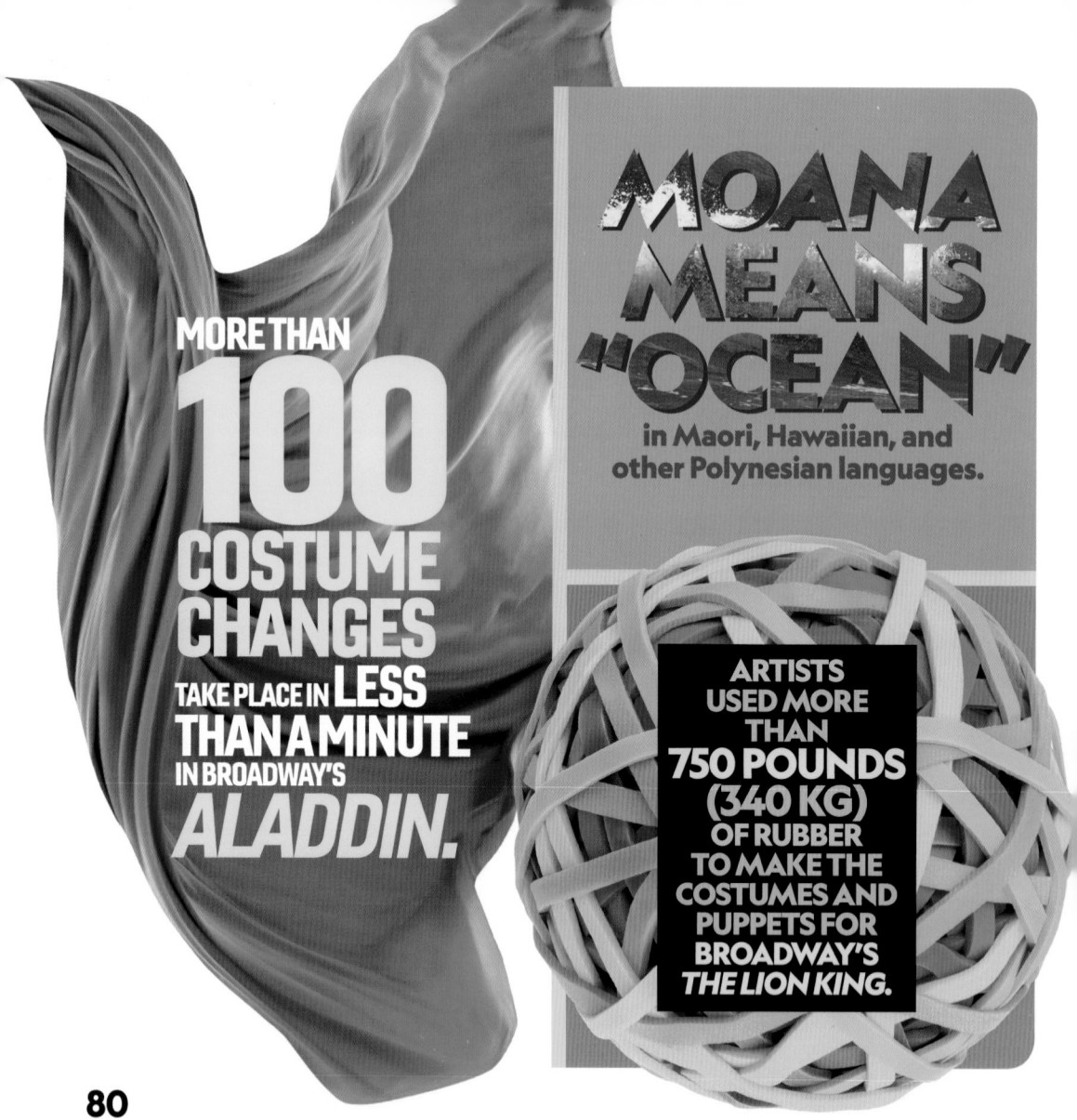
MORE THAN
100
COSTUME CHANGES
TAKE PLACE IN LESS THAN A MINUTE
IN BROADWAY'S
ALADDIN.
MOANA MEANS "OCEAN"
in Maori, Hawaiian, and other Polynesian languages.
ARTISTS USED MORE THAN
750 POUNDS (340 KG)
OF RUBBER TO MAKE THE COSTUMES AND PUPPETS FOR BROADWAY'S
THE LION KING.

Animators for *Bolt* (2008) had a pet hamster named **Doink!** that helped them model the movements for the animated hamster Rhino.

Anika Noni Rose, who voiced TIANA in *The Princess and the Frog* (2009), asked that her character be LEFT-HANDED, JUST LIKE HER.

That's weird!

FOR *SECRETS OF THE WHALES* (2021), SCIENTISTS COLLECTED MORE DATA ON THESE SEA MAMMALS THAN THE HUBBLE TELESCOPE GATHERS ABOUT SPACE IN A YEAR.

There are more than
10,000 items
in the antiques mall
that Woody wanders
in Toy Story 4
(2019).
EACH OF THE MORE THAN
270 FOOD ITEMS
THAT APPEAR IN RATATOUILLE
(2007) WAS PREPARED IN A
REAL KITCHEN AND EATEN.

Rafiki—the name of the mandrill in *The Lion King* (1994)—means "friend" in Swahili.
An actor **growled** into a trash can to **create** the lion roars for the film.

THE PUMBAA COSTUME IN BROADWAY'S *THE LION KING* WEIGHS 45 POUNDS (20 KG) AND IS WORN LIKE A
BACKPACK.

Only materials that would have been available on **Pacific islands** were used to design the characters' clothes in ***Moana* (2016).**

IN 1933, MICKEY MOUSE REPORTEDLY RECEIVED **800,000 FAN LETTERS,** THE MOST OF ANY HOLLYWOOD STAR AT THE TIME.

In 2005, **LUCKY**, a nine-foot (2.7-m)-tall, **450-pound** (204-kg) **dinosaur**—Disney's first free-roaming Audio-Animatronics® figure—walked **DinoLand U.S.A.** in **Disney's Animal Kingdom**.

The 82-foot (25-m)-tall fireplace in **DISNEY'S WILDERNESS LODGE** mimics the layers of the Grand Canyon, which represent **1.6 BILLION YEARS OF GEOLOGIC HISTORY.**

MAYOR LIONHEART FROM ZOOTOPIA (2016) WAS PARTLY INSPIRED BY THE LION KING'S MUFASA.
AROUND HALLOWEEN, MORE THAN
300 SCULPTED PUMPKINS
LINE MAIN STREET, U.S.A. AT DISNEYLAND—AND NO TWO ARE ALIKE.

Walt Disney decided to make a Winnie the Pooh film after hearing his children giggle while listening to A. A. Milne's Winnie-the-Pooh stories.
The Banks' house in Broadway's *Mary Poppins* weighed 20 tons (18 t).
A RECORDING OF NIAGARA FALLS, WHERE 3,160 TONS (2,867 T) OF WATER GUSH OVER THE EDGE EVERY SECOND, CREATED THE SOUND OF THE WIND ON EARTH IN *WALL·E* (2008).

The **venomous** Amazonian **giant centipede,** which can grow to **a foot (30 cm) long,** was the model for the character of **Dean Hardscrabble** in *Monsters University* (2013).

The gargoyles of Notre Dame Cathedral partly inspired the Beast's castle in *Beauty and the Beast* (1991).
In the film, Belle is the only character in her village who wears the color blue.

Finnick's name in *Zootopia* (2016) is a play on his species, the fennec fox.

THE MAKEUP FOR EACH OF BLACKBEARD'S ZOMBIE CREW IN PIRATES OF THE CARIBBEAN: ON STRANGER TIDES (2011) TOOK AN AVERAGE OF THREE AND A HALF HOURS TO COMPLETE.
THE LARGE MR. POTATO HEAD outside Toy Story Midway Mania! at Disney California Adventure can say more lines than any other Disney-created AUDIO-ANIMATRONICS® FIGURE.
In one year, each Radiator Springs Racers ride vehicle travels about 36,000 miles (57,936 km)—that's equal to almost one and a half trips around the Equator.

The **23** on the 623 trolley at Disney California Adventure refers to **1923**, the year Walt Disney **arrived** in Los Angeles.

The carvings above The Little Mermaid ~ Ariel's Undersea Adventure at Disney California Adventure depict Ariel's six older sisters: **Aquata, Andrina, Arista, Attina, Adella,** and **Alana.**

The Anaheim Fire Department thought the burning city scene in Pirates of the Caribbean looked so real that they were reluctant to approve the ride.

You can buy a soap pump that dispenses soap in the shape of Mickey Mouse's head.

ONE WOMAN OWNS MORE THAN **10,000 ITEMS OF MICKEY MOUSE MEMORABILIA**— THE WORLD'S LARGEST COLLECTION.

The attraction "it's a small world" is found at Disney parks on three continents—North America, Europe, and Asia—so its theme song is always playing somewhere on Earth.

More than 3,600 colorful plants create Mickey Mouse's floral face at the entrance to Disneyland.

AT CLUB COOL IN WORLD CELEBRATION AT EPCOT, YOU CAN TASTE-TEST SODAS FROM AROUND THE WORLD.

CAPUCHIN MONKEYS AT THE LOS ANGELES ZOO WERE PART OF THE INSPIRATION FOR ABU IN *ALADDIN* (1992).

One person's sole job at Disneyland is to take care of King Arthur Carrousel's 68 horses, many of which are more than 100 years old.
The windows and interior handles of the monorail cars at Tokyo Disney Resort are shaped like Mickey Mouse's head.

SUMMIT PLUMMET WATERSLIDE AT DISNEY'S BLIZZARD BEACH WATER PARK SENDS RIDERS DOWN A 12-STORY-TALL DROP AT UP TO 60 MILES AN HOUR (96 KM/H).

THE TREASURE SCENE IN DISNEYLAND'S PIRATES OF THE CARIBBEAN ATTRACTION CONTAINS ABOUT **400,000 COINS.**

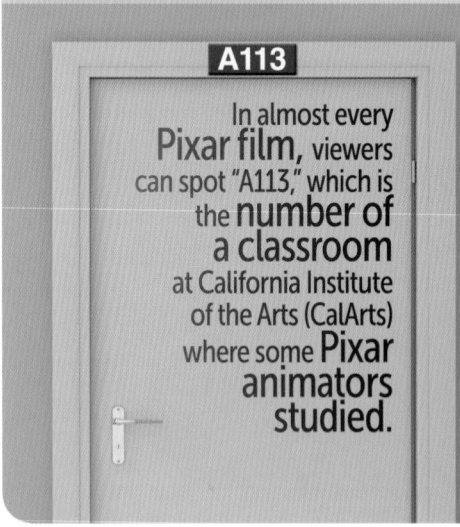

In almost every **Pixar film,** viewers can spot "A113," which is the **number of a classroom** at California Institute of the Arts (CalArts) where some **Pixar animators studied.**

TO HELP ANIMATORS STAGE THE ACTION FOR ***SNOW WHITE AND THE SEVEN DWARFS*** (1937), A DISNEY ARTIST CREATED A FULL-SCALE MODEL OF THE **DWARFS' COTTAGE.**

MICKEY MOUSE'S BIRTHDAY IS NOVEMBER 18, THE DAY THAT **"STEAMBOAT WILLIE"** (1928), HIS AND MINNIE'S FIRST CARTOON, PREMIERED.

THE MOTION OF A RATTLESNAKE STRIKING WAS THE INSPIRATION FOR THE DRAGON MOVING TO ATTACK PRINCE PHILLIP IN *SLEEPING BEAUTY* (1959).

NATIONAL DONALD DUCK DAY IS JUNE 9, THE DAY HIS FIRST CARTOON, "THE WISE LITTLE HEN" (1934), PREMIERED.
Much of "it's a small world" was designed to look like a child's papier-mâché art project.
THE FIRST ANIMAL BORN AT DISNEY'S ANIMAL KINGDOM WAS A KUDU, A LARGE AFRICAN ANTELOPE.

Some popcorn carts at Disneyland feature "Roastie-Toasties"— dolls that rotate the popcorn drums.

In the "It's Tough to be a Bug!" 3D film at Disney's Animal Kingdom, visitors smell the stench of a stink bug.
It takes 70,000 "perfume" pellets to create the smell.

THE DESIGN OF THE LIFEBOATS ON DISNEY CRUISE LINE SHIPS IS INSPIRED BY THE COLOR OF MICKEY MOUSE'S SHOES.

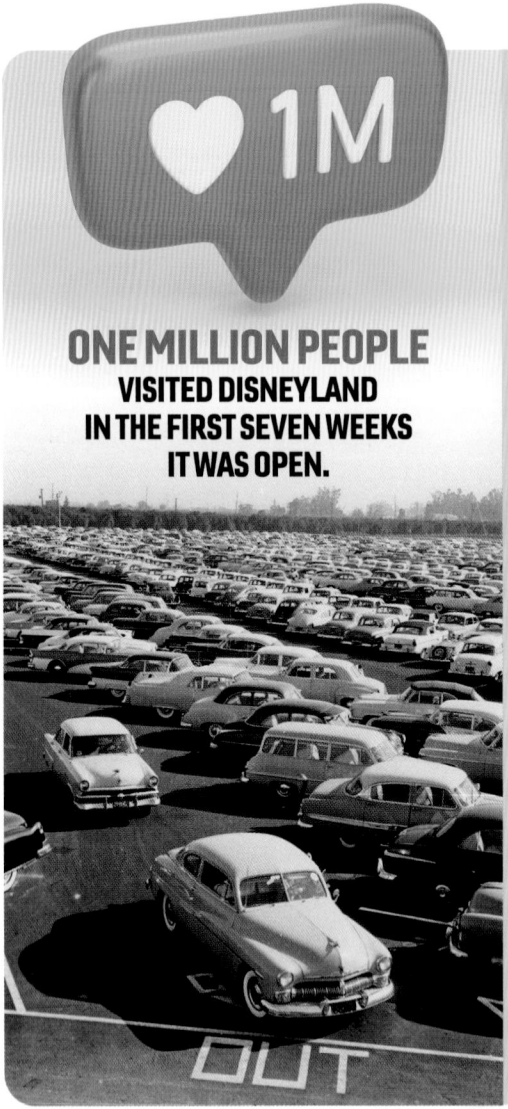

ONE MILLION PEOPLE VISITED DISNEYLAND IN THE FIRST SEVEN WEEKS IT WAS OPEN.

The Guardians of the Galaxy: Cosmic Rewind coaster at EPCOT includes a backward launch, and the ride vehicles turn 360 degrees.

As a boy, Walt Disney drew on anything he could find—even toilet paper.

In *The Little Mermaid* (1989), Sebastian the crab's full name is
Horatio
Thelonious
Ignacious
Crustaceous
Sebastian.

THE singing busts IN THE HAUNTED MANSION ARE NAMED ...

ROLO RUMKIN

UNCLE THEODORE

COUSIN ALGERNON
NED NUB
PHINEAS P. POCK

Cinderella's dress
transforming
into a ball gown
was said to be
Walt Disney's favorite
piece of animation.

Walt Disney's pocket on the "Storytellers" statue in Disney California Adventure
holds the *Kansas City Star* newspaper—a nod to the city where
Walt opened his first animation studio.
At the France pavilion in EPCOT, some of the manhole covers feature Remy from *Ratatouille* (2007), a reference to the rat's arrival in Paris via the sewers.
The Forbidden Mountain at Disney's Animal Kingdom is the tallest "mountain" in Florida, at almost 200 feet (61 m).

WHEN THE
JUNGLE CRUISE
WAS BUILT AT DISNEYLAND,
ORANGE TREES WERE PLANTED
UPSIDE DOWN BECAUSE THEIR
ROOTS LOOKED LIKE
A TYPE OF TREE
FROM AFRICA.
More than half the U.S. population watched the television broadcast of Disneyland's opening day on July 17, 1955.
Donald Duck has an asteroid named after him.

The movements of **Baymax,** the inflatable robot in ***Big Hero 6*** (2014), were based on those of **baby penguins.**

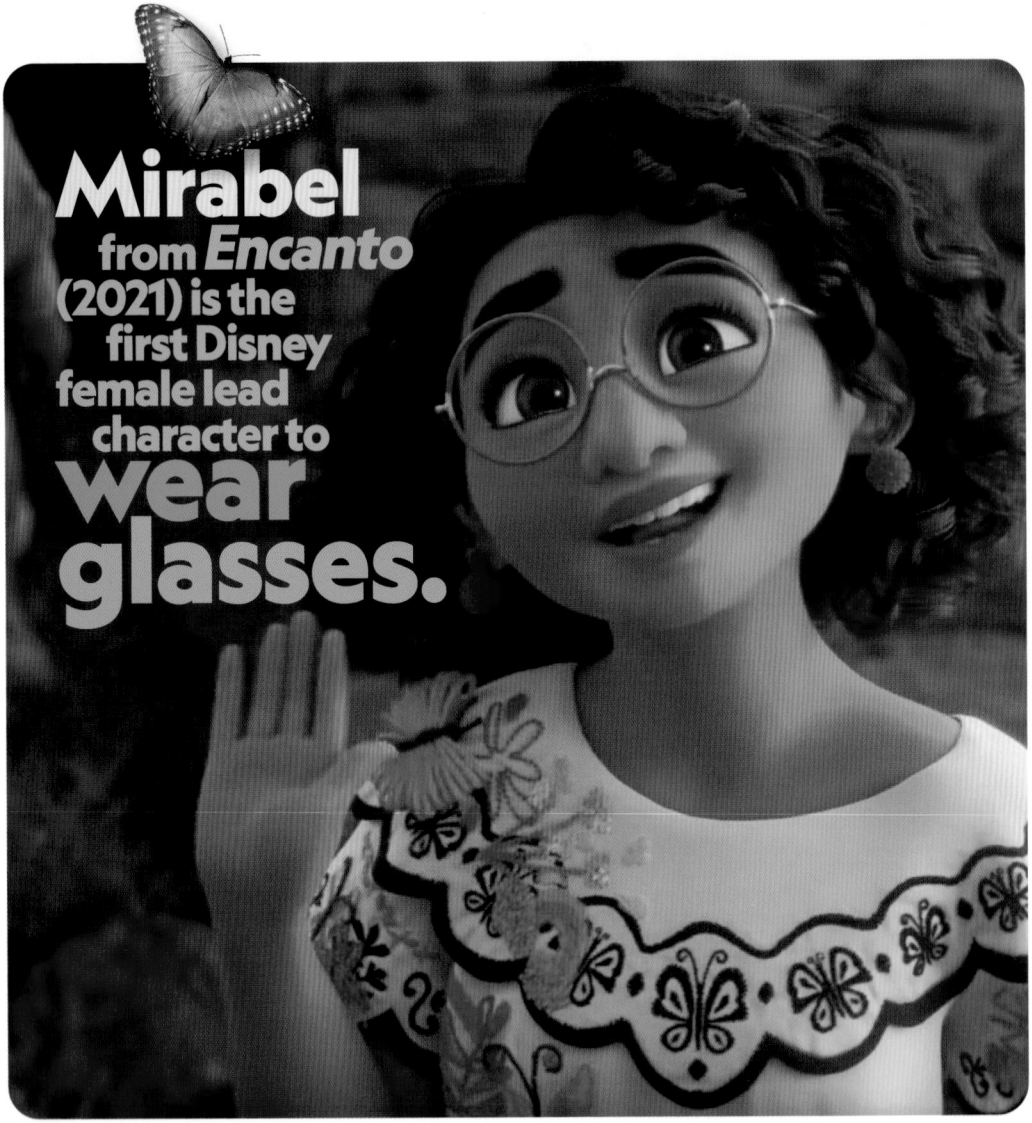

Mirabel from *Encanto* (2021) is the first Disney female lead character to **wear glasses.**

More than **30 million blossoms** bloom at the EPCOT International Flower & Garden Festival.

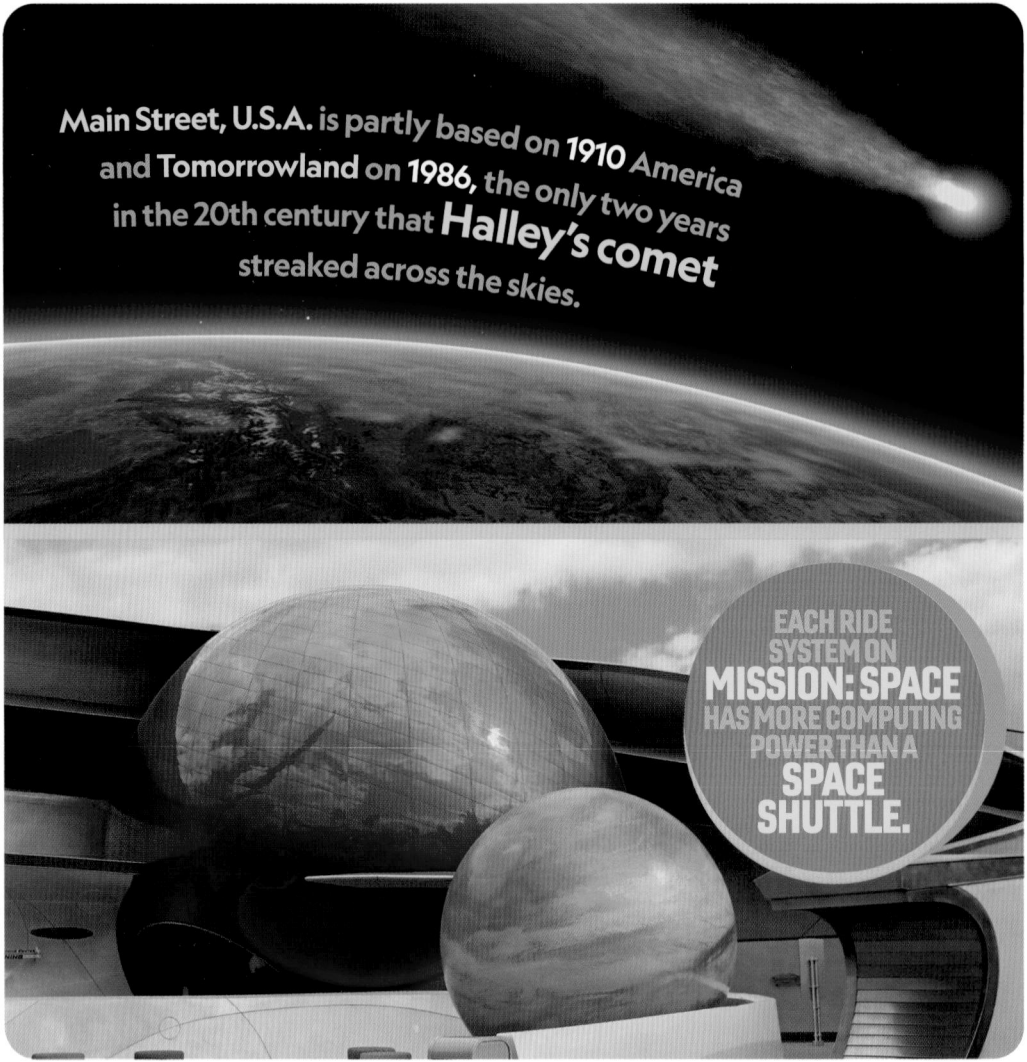
Main Street, U.S.A. is partly based on 1910 America and Tomorrowland on 1986, the only two years in the 20th century that Halley's comet streaked across the skies.
EACH RIDE SYSTEM ON MISSION: SPACE HAS MORE COMPUTING POWER THAN A SPACE SHUTTLE.

WALT DISNEY LOVED TRAINS SO MUCH THAT HE HAD ONE IN HIS BACKYARD BIG ENOUGH FOR HIM TO RIDE.

Sleeping Beauty Castle opened in 1955, more than three years before the release of *Sleeping Beauty* (1959).

Gustave Eiffel's blueprints were used to create the Eiffel Tower in the France pavilion at **EPCOT.**

BRUCE, THE GREAT WHITE SHARK IN *FINDING NEMO* (2003), HAS **202 TEETH** THAT ARE EACH ANIMATABLE.

MICKEY MOUSE is called **Topolino** in Italy and **Musse Pigg** in Sweden.

SANTA SHARES 300 POUNDS (136 KG) OF GINGERBREAD COOKIES ON EACH DISNEY CRUISE LINE SHIP DURING THE HOLIDAYS.

KEVIN in Up (2009) is a combination of many birds, including a
cassowary,
an ostrich,
and a monal pheasant.

GOLDEN MONKEYS, ASIAN LANGURS, AND PREHISTORIC *GIGANTOPITHECUS*—THE BIGGEST PRIMATE THAT EVER LIVED—WERE AMONG THE INSPIRATIONS FOR THE **Yeti in Expedition Everest** – LEGEND OF THE FORBIDDEN MOUNTAIN.

To save time, animators didn't create toes for any of the human characters in *Ratatouille* (2007).

THE **SOLE ANIMATOR** ON THE FIRST SHORT FILM FEATURING MICKEY MOUSE CREATED AS MANY AS 700 DRAWINGS A DAY.

ANIMATORS CREATED ALMOST 13,000 INDIVIDUAL CORALS FOR NEMO AND HIS FRIENDS TO SWIM THROUGH IN *FINDING NEMO* (2003).

To make Miguel's homemade guitar more realistically childlike, the director of *Coco* (2017) asked his son to design it.

Some of the cobblestones in the streets of *Coco's* (2017) Land of the Dead are bone-shaped.

THE **will-o'-the-wisps** THAT BECKON MERIDA IN *BRAVE* (2012) ARE INSPIRED BY SCOTTISH LORE.

SWAMP GASES CREATED **little blue lights** THAT PEOPLE FOLLOWED, THINKING THEY WERE **FAIRIES.**

The Pizza Planet truck, which first appeared in Toy Story (1995), appears in almost every Pixar movie.

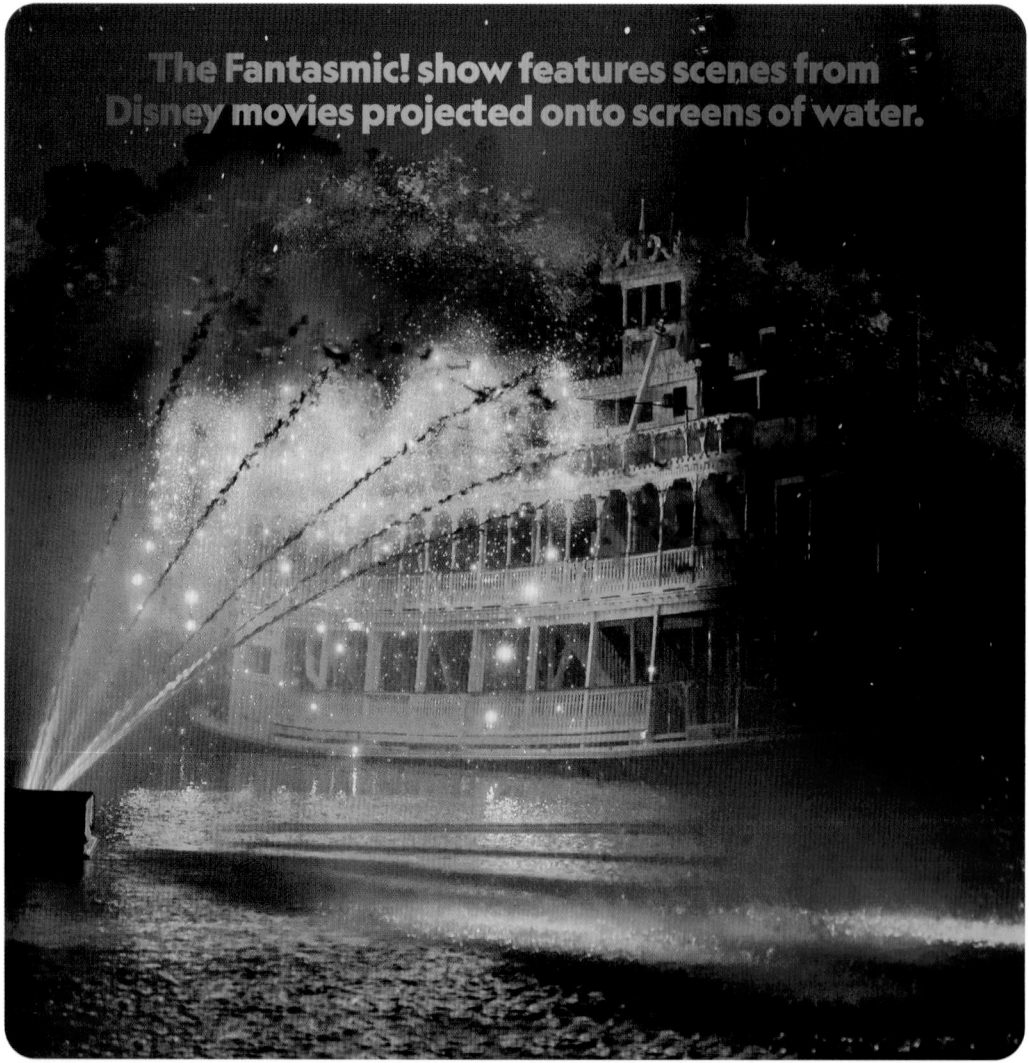

The Fantasmic! show features scenes from Disney movies projected onto screens of water.

There is a restaurant inside the Pirates of the Caribbean attraction at Disneyland.

IN *SOUL* (2020), THE NUMBER OF SOULS WHO LEAVE THE GREAT BEFORE FOR EARTH IS BASED ON REAL STATISTICS:

About four people are born each second around the world.

Guests of Disneyland Resort Hotels can sign up for an EARLY MORNING POWER WALK through Disney California Adventure before the park opens.

30

Mickey Mouse wears more than 200 outfits at Disneyland Paris.

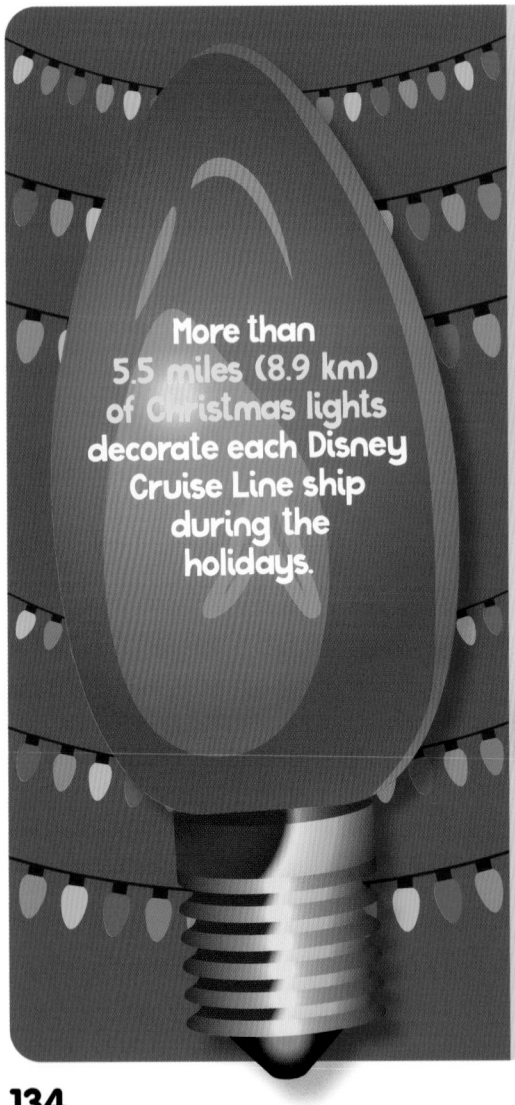

More than 5.5 miles (8.9 km) of Christmas lights decorate each Disney Cruise Line ship during the holidays.

Costuming teams at Disneyland Paris ordered **18 miles** (29 km) of fabric in just one year.

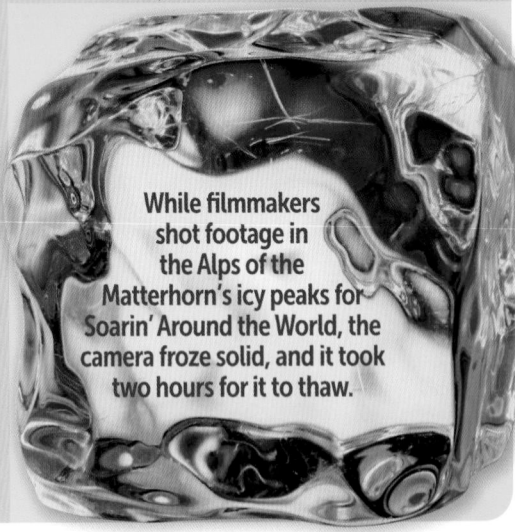

While filmmakers shot footage in the Alps of the Matterhorn's icy peaks for Soarin' Around the World, the camera froze solid, and it took two hours for it to thaw.

WHEN CREATING THE CHARACTER OF ARLO FOR *THE GOOD DINOSAUR* (2015), ANIMATORS VISITED A ZOO TO WATCH HOW ELEPHANTS—ANOTHER HEAVY, FOUR-FOOTED ANIMAL—MOVED.

A plaque near **Sleeping Beauty Castle** marks the spot of a **time capsule** that contains mementos from Disneyland's **40th anniversary** celebration in 1995.

At the opening of **"it's a small world"** at Disneyland in 1966, **Walt Disney** and a group of children poured water collected from **Earth's rivers and oceans** into the ride's canal.

Grizzly Peak at Disney California Adventure is in the form of a California grizzly bear—the state animal.

The main courtyard of Disney's **Hollywood Studios** forms a **big Hidden Mickey** that can only be seen from above.

The actor who played the **Beast in *Beauty and the Beast*** (2017) walked on stilts and wore a **40-POUND (18-KG) SUIT** with movement sensors to create the computer-generated character.

Walt Disney originally wanted **real animals** to entertain guests on the **Jungle Cruise.**

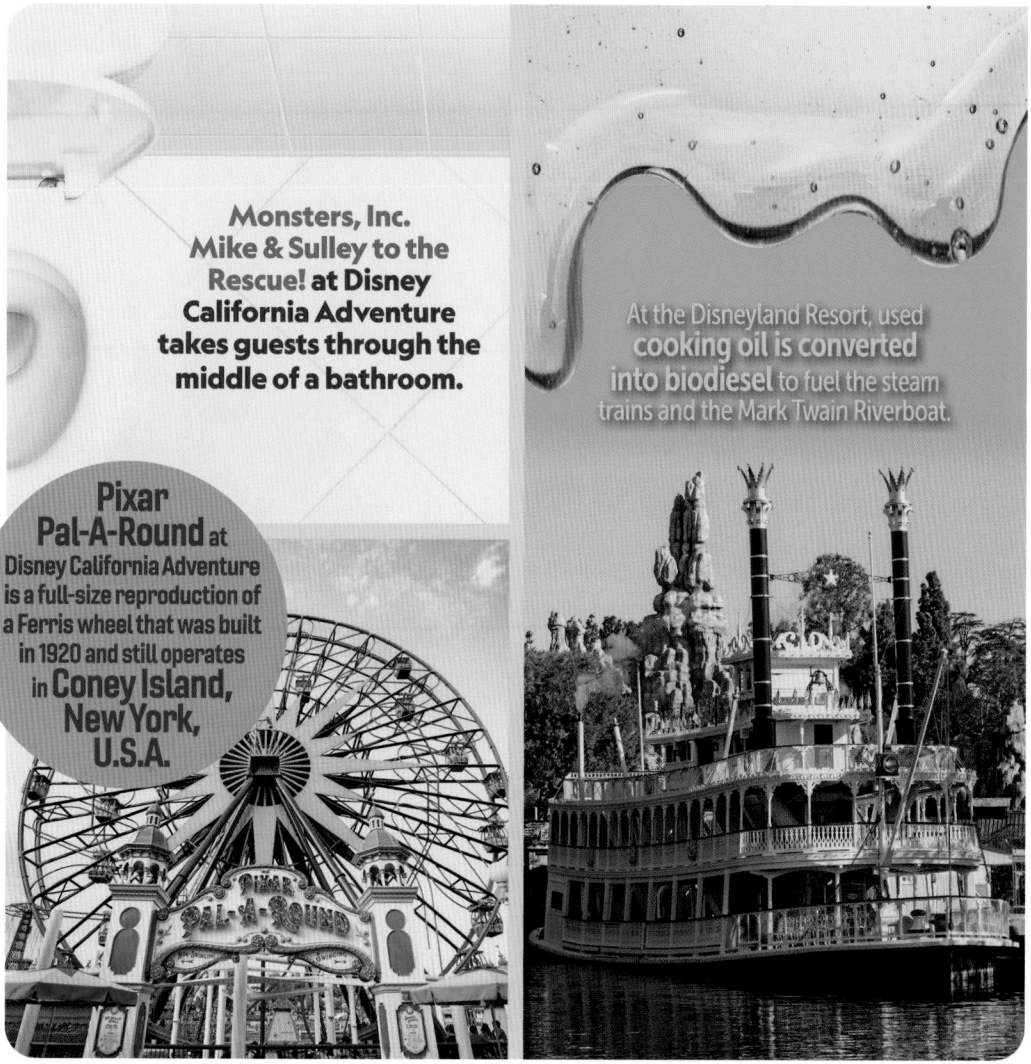

Monsters, Inc. Mike & Sulley to the Rescue! at Disney California Adventure takes guests through the middle of a bathroom.

Pixar Pal-A-Round at Disney California Adventure is a full-size reproduction of a Ferris wheel that was built in 1920 and still operates in **Coney Island, New York, U.S.A.**

At the Disneyland Resort, used **cooking oil is converted into biodiesel** to fuel the steam trains and the Mark Twain Riverboat.

The ***T. rex* family** in *The Good Dinosaur* (2015) **are ranchers,** so animators gave them lower bodies that move like **galloping horses** and upper bodies of **riding cowboys.**

To make the New York City scenes realistic, *Soul* (2020) animators included black spots on the sidewalks to look like wads of walked-over chewing gum.

NORTH AMERICA
ASIA
EUROPE
Italy
AFRICA
EUROPE
Maranello
ITALY
Adriatic Sea
Tyrrhenian Sea
Mediterranean Sea
AFRICA
Sulley
in Monsters, Inc. (2001) has more than five million individual hairs on his body.
IN CARS (2006), LUIGI'S LICENSE PLATE NUMBER,
44.5-10.8
REPRESENTS THE LATITUDE AND LONGITUDE OF FERRARI HEADQUARTERS IN MARANELLO, ITALY.

***Lilo & Stitch* (2002) animators consulted Hawaiian hula**

dancers to make sure that Lilo's hula steps were accurate.

For ***Onward*** **(2020), animators danced with their arms tied behind their backs to create footage for the moving pair of pants.**

Paradise Falls
in *Up* (2009) is based on
Venezuela's
Angel Falls,
the world's tallest
waterfall.

The manatees at The Seas with Nemo & Friends at EPCOT eat more than **100 heads of lettuce a day.**

Gino, a silverback gorilla at Disney's Animal Kingdom, celebrated his 41st birthday with a cake made of alfalfa, banana leaves, and sweet potato frosting.
Two actors who voiced Mickey Mouse and Minnie Mouse were married to each other in real life.
WHEN WALT DISNEY WAS THINKING ABOUT A NAME FOR WHAT WOULD BECOME DISNEYLAND, HE CONSIDERED CALLING IT "MICKEY MOUSE PARK."

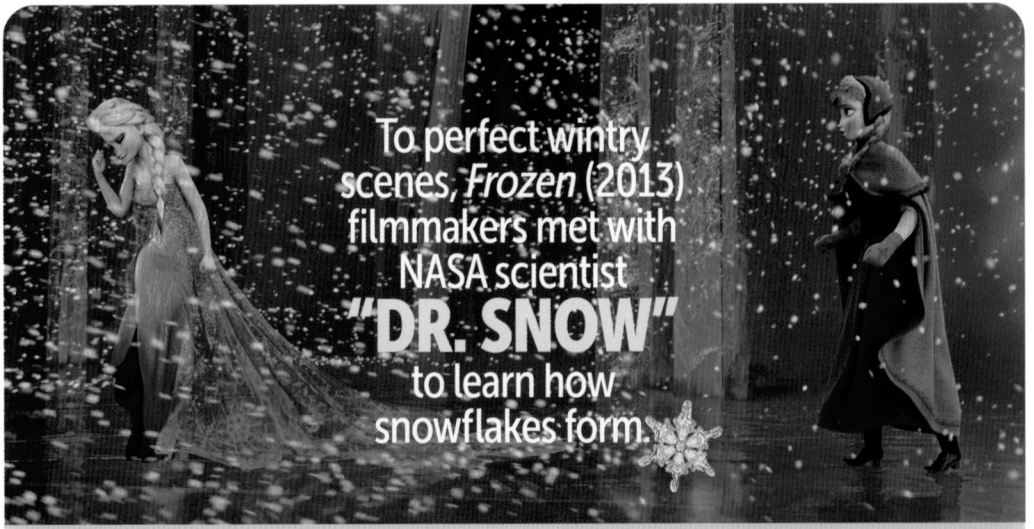

To perfect wintry scenes, *Frozen* (2013) filmmakers met with NASA scientist **"DR. SNOW"** to learn how snowflakes form.

Québec City's **HÔTEL DE GLACE,** where you can **sleep in a room made of snow and ice,** was an inspiration for Elsa's ice palace in *Frozen* (2013).

REINDEER use their hind legs to scratch their ears—a trait that *Frozen* (2013) animators used for the character of **SVEN.**

Disneynature filmmakers **TRAVELED ACROSS A GLACIER FOR 10 DAYS** to transport the sled-mounted mobile camp they lived in while filming the documentary ***POLAR BEAR*** (2022).

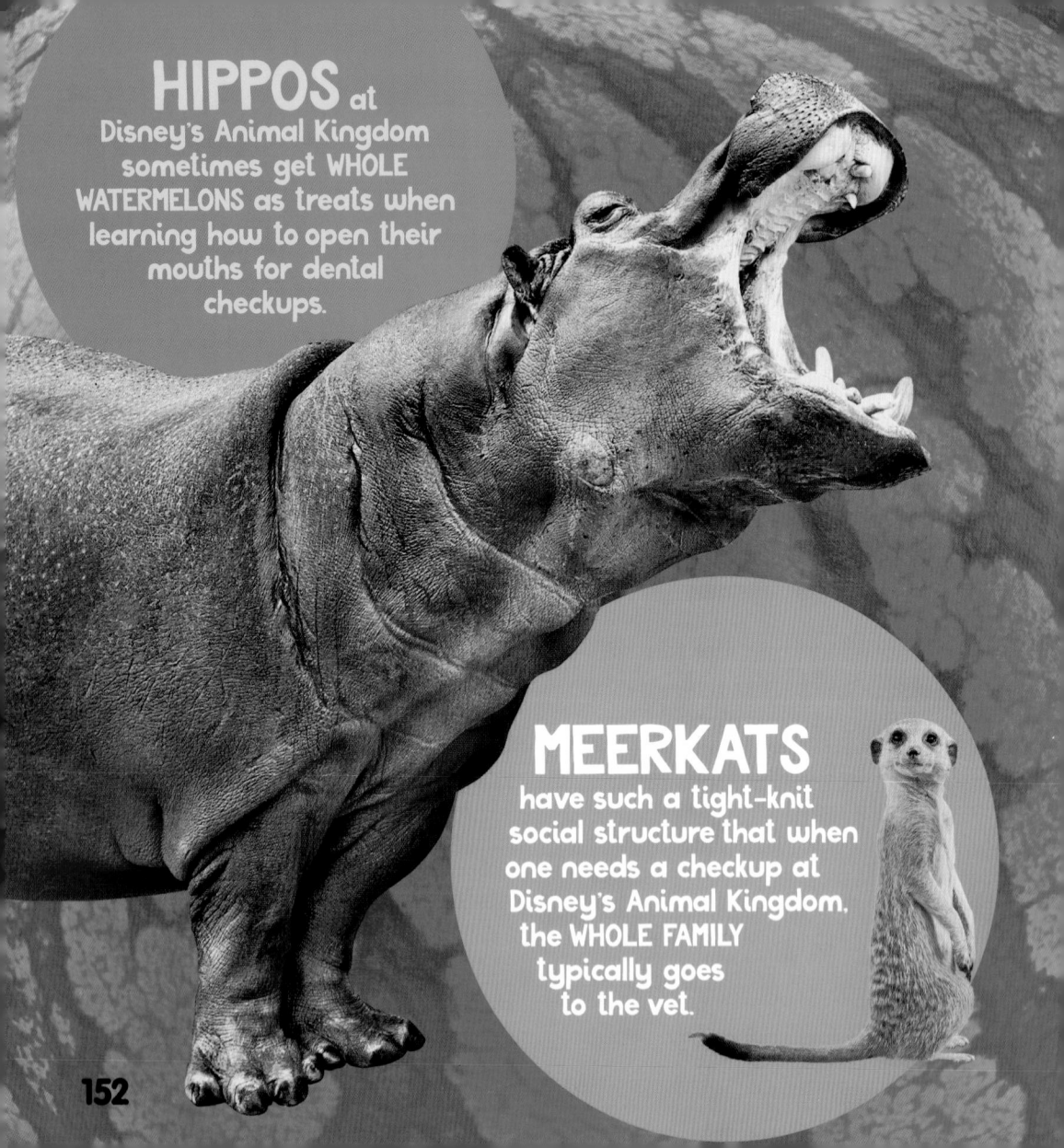

HIPPOS at Disney's Animal Kingdom sometimes get WHOLE WATERMELONS as treats when learning how to open their mouths for dental checkups.

MEERKATS have such a tight-knit social structure that when one needs a checkup at Disney's Animal Kingdom, the WHOLE FAMILY typically goes to the vet.

Mirrors are sometimes used in the **LESSER FLAMINGO** exhibits at Disney's Animal Kingdom to create the illusion of the larger flocks that these birds would be part of during breeding season in the wild.

ROCK 'N' ROLLER COASTER STARRING
AEROSMITH
WAS THE FIRST COASTER AT WALT DISNEY WORLD
TO TAKE GUESTS UPSIDE DOWN.
PHINEAS,
EZRA,
AND GUS are the names of the HITCHHIKING GHOSTS who try to catch a ride out of the Haunted Mansion.

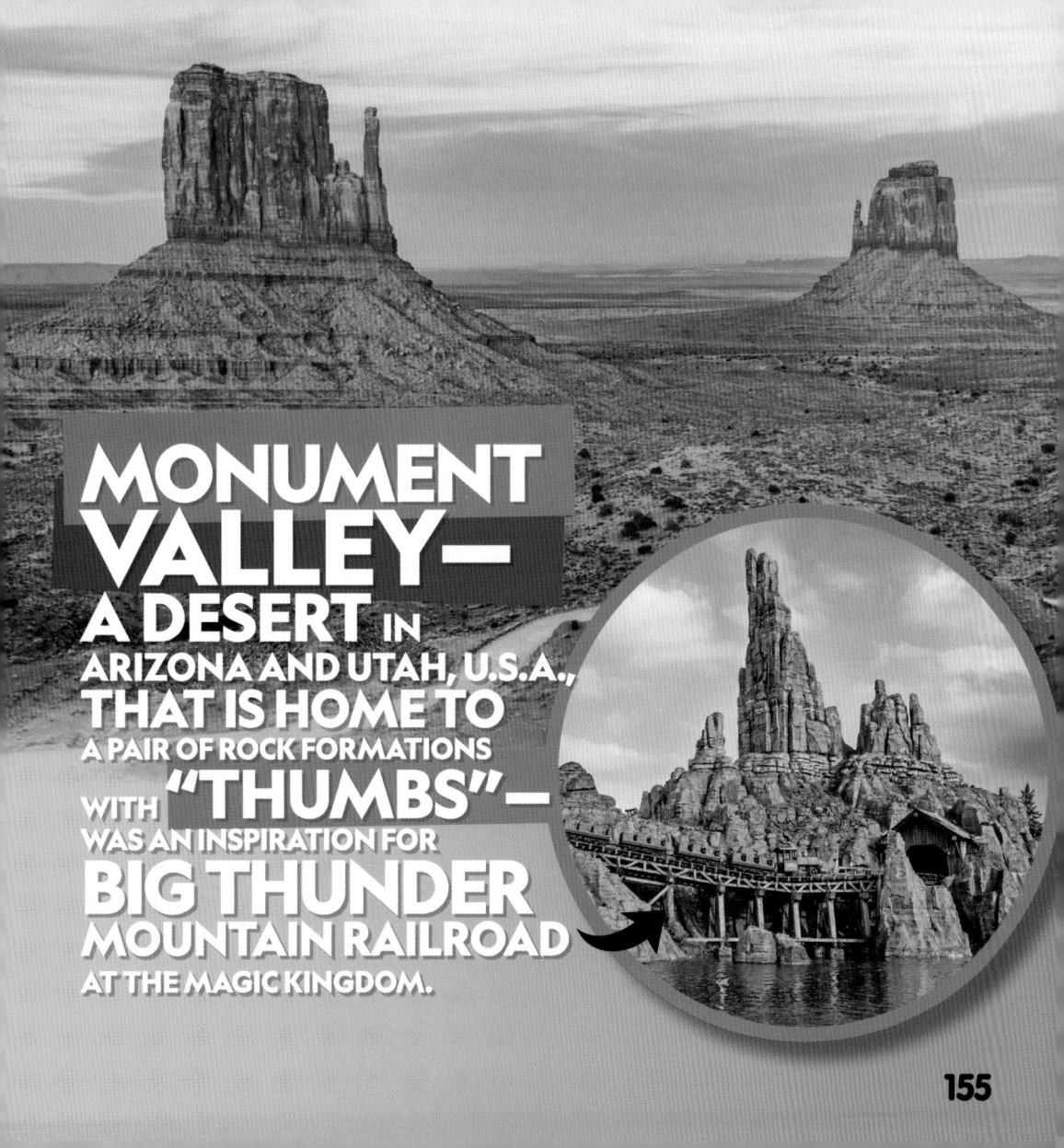

MONUMENT VALLEY—A DESERT IN ARIZONA AND UTAH, U.S.A., THAT IS HOME TO A PAIR OF ROCK FORMATIONS WITH "THUMBS"—WAS AN INSPIRATION FOR BIG THUNDER MOUNTAIN RAILROAD AT THE MAGIC KINGDOM.

Disneynature filmmakers **wore penguin masks** to blend in with **Earth's largest Adélie colony**—more than **one million birds in Antarctica**—while shooting the documentary *Penguins* (2019).

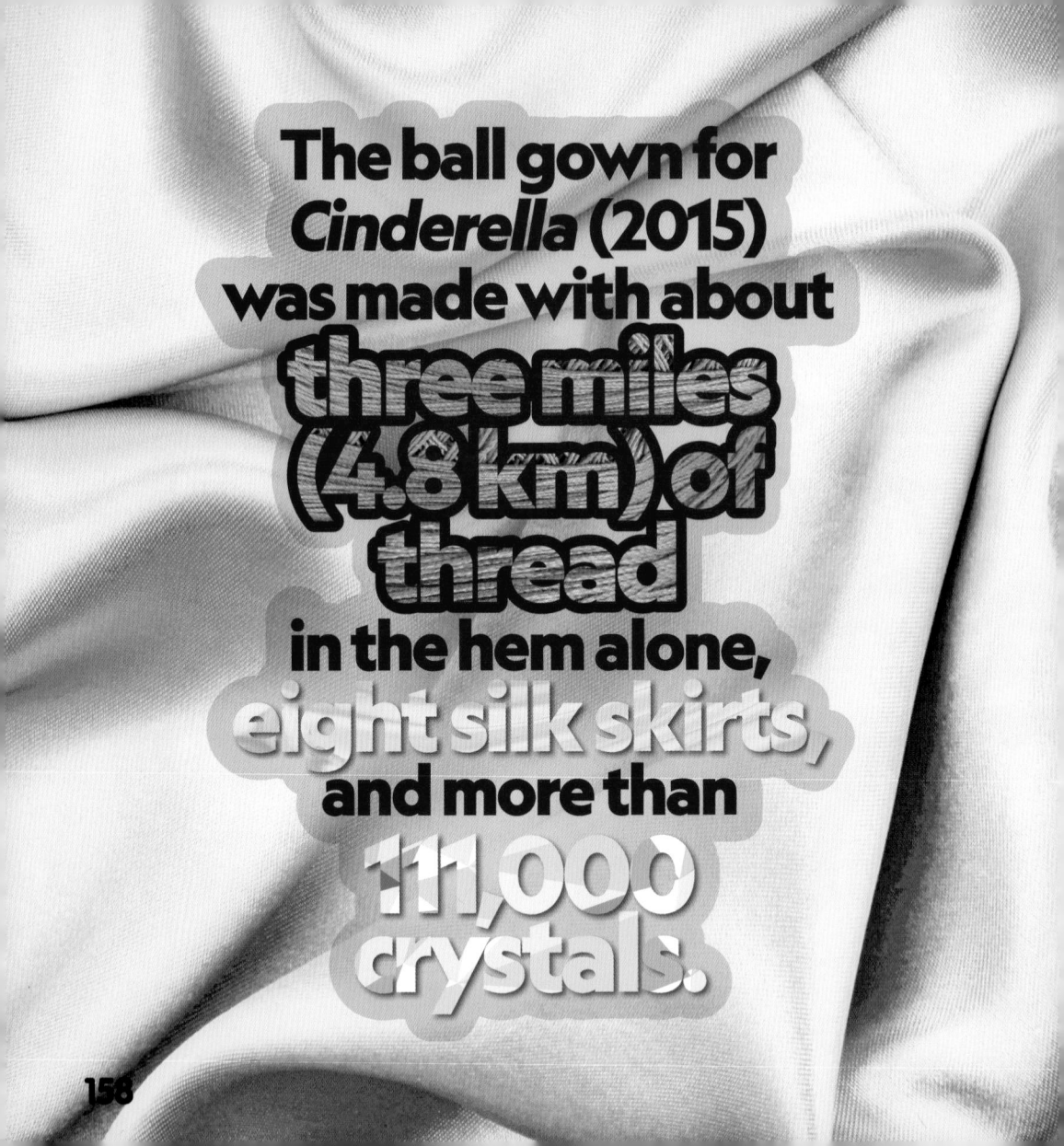
The ball gown for
Cinderella (2015)
was made with about
three miles
(4.8 km) of
thread
in the hem alone,
eight silk skirts,
and more than
111,000
crystals.

THE ACTRESS WHO PLAYED CINDERELLA DID NOT WALK IN THE CRYSTAL HEELS CREATED FOR THE FILM—
SHE WORE LEATHER SHOES AND A COMPUTER MADE THEM APPEAR AS THE GLASS SLIPPERS.

The **murals in Cinderella Castle** at the Magic Kingdom are made with hundreds of thousands of glass tiles in **500 colors,** including a **red shade** made just for Cinderella's **jealous stepsister.**

The window shutters in Liberty Square at the Magic Kingdom **HANG AT AN ANGLE,** because upper hinges in COLONIAL AMERICA were often made of leather straps, which made the shutters tilt.

Each clamshell ride vehicle on The Little Mermaid ~ **Ariel's Undersea Adventure** at Disney California Adventure weighs as much as **4,360 average-size clams.**

A police escort helps transport about 100 tons (91 t) of holiday decorations to Main Street, U.S.A. at the Magic Kingdom each year.
During the holidays, each of the more than 300 dolls in "it's a small world" at Disneyland is dressed in a special costume or accessory.

FILMMAKERS STUDIED THE LIONS AT DISNEY'S ANIMAL KINGDOM TO CREATE *THE LION KING*'S COMPUTER-GENERATED ONES.

SPECIAL "GROOM" ARTISTS CREATED THE REALISTIC LOOK OF THE ANIMALS' FUR IN *THE LION KING* (2019).

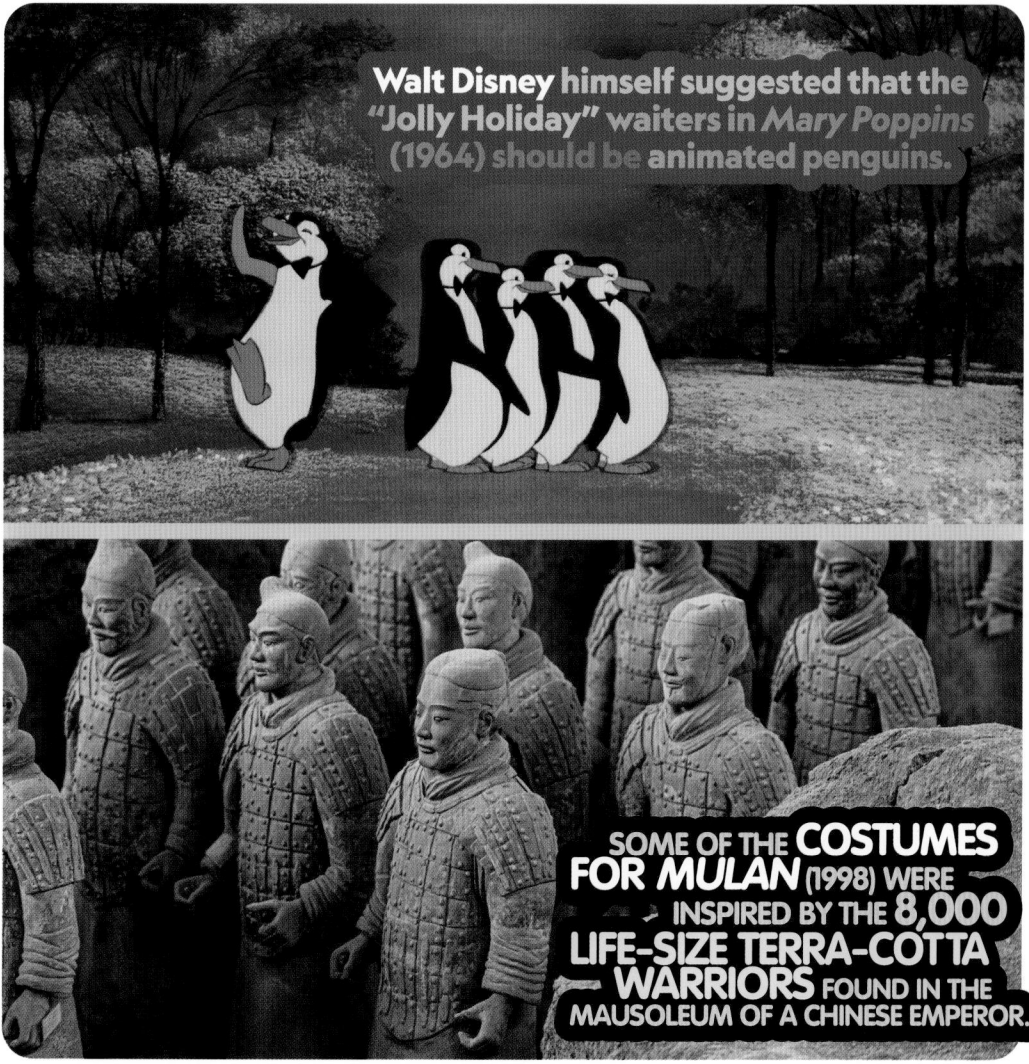
Walt Disney himself suggested that the "Jolly Holiday" waiters in *Mary Poppins* (1964) should be animated penguins.
SOME OF THE COSTUMES FOR *MULAN* (1998) WERE INSPIRED BY THE 8,000 LIFE-SIZE TERRA-COTTA WARRIORS FOUND IN THE MAUSOLEUM OF A CHINESE EMPEROR.

COOL

To make the posters that hang in the middle school in ***Turning Red* (2022)** look as if they were

drawn by middle schoolers,

some artists changed their **grip on their pen.**

IMAGINEERS MIXED CONCRETE WITH STONES, DIRT, AND TWIGS TO CREATE THE **BUMPY ROAD** FOR THE KILIMANJARO SAFARIS IN DISNEY'S ANIMAL KINGDOM.

An artist who helped **restore the stained-glass windows for Notre Dame Cathedral** also designed the windows for Sleeping Beauty Castle at Disneyland Paris.

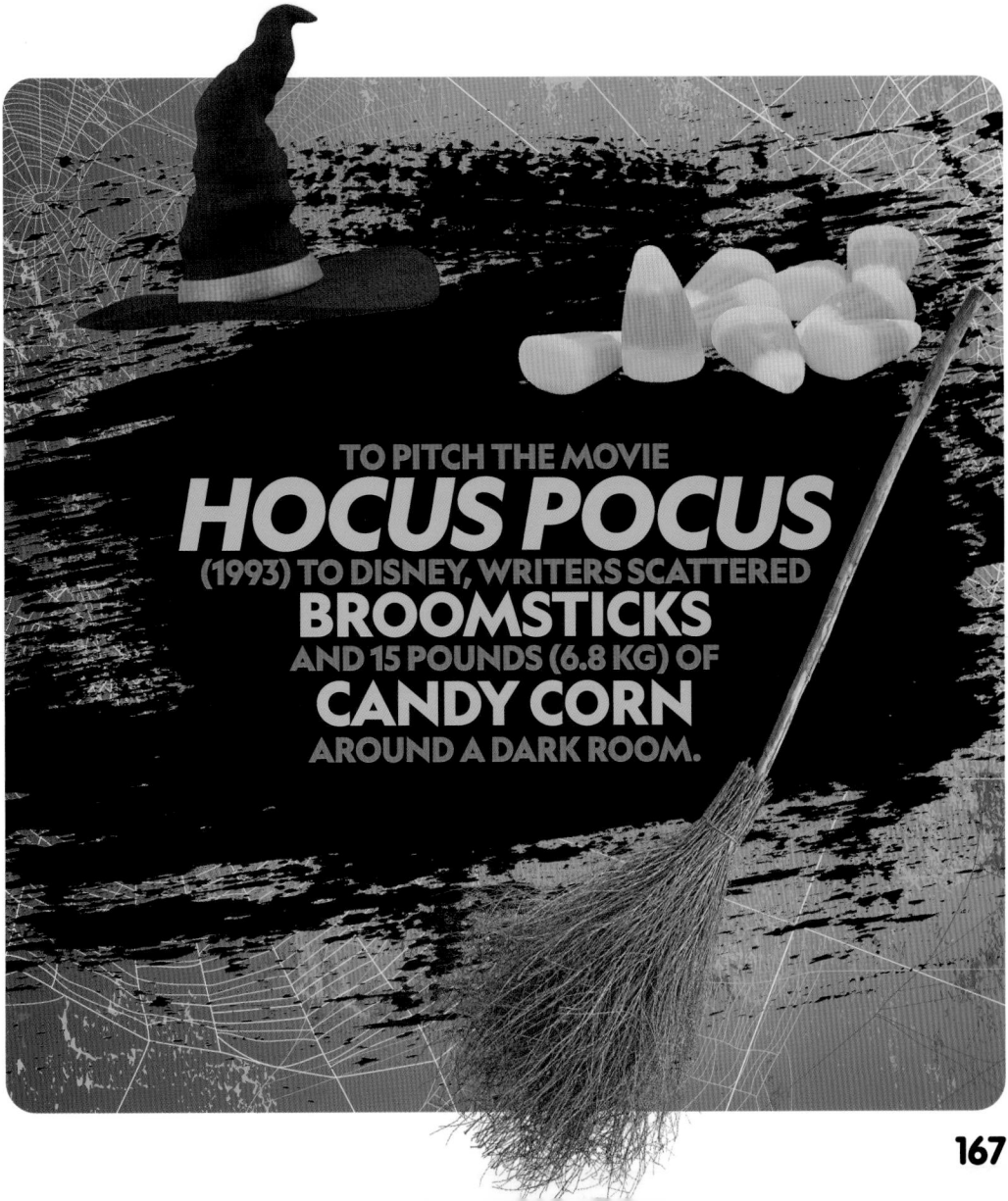

TO PITCH THE MOVIE
HOCUS POCUS
(1993) TO DISNEY, WRITERS SCATTERED
BROOMSTICKS
AND 15 POUNDS (6.8 KG) OF
CANDY CORN
AROUND A DARK ROOM.

In *Wreck-It Ralph* (2012), the high score of the Fix-It Felix Jr. video game, 120501, refers to Walt Disney's birthday: December 5, 1901.
SCIENTISTS SUGGESTED ASTROTURF FOR THE HABITAT OF HANK, THE OCTOPUS IN *FINDING DORY* (2016)—IT WOULD PREVENT HIS ESCAPE BECAUSE HIS SUCKERS COULDN'T STICK TO IT.
The tree house in Swiss Family Robinson (1960) was built in a 200-foot (61-m)-tall saman tree in Tobago.

THE NAUTILUS, CAPTAIN NEMO'S SHIP IN 20,000 LEAGUES UNDER THE SEA (1954), WAS DESIGNED TO RESEMBLE A CROSS BETWEEN ...
AN ALLIGATOR
AND A SHARK.
The clicking steps of the pet Cockroach in WALL•E (2008) are a recording of handcuffs jingling.

1,428
Swarovski diamonds
were sewn into just
ONE PAIR OF
COSTUME PANTS
worn in Broadway's Aladdin.

Prince Charming does not have a given name in *Cinderella* (1950).

SCIENTISTS NAMED ONE SPECIES OF A TINY FAIRY FLY *TINKERBELLA NANA*, AFTER TWO CHARACTERS IN *PETER PAN* (1953).

THE TRUCKS GUESTS RIDE ON KILIMANJARO SAFARIS AT DISNEY'S ANIMAL KINGDOM WEIGH AS MUCH AS **10 TONS (9 T)—THAT'S HEAVIER THAN AN AFRICAN ELEPHANT.**

The gibbons at Disney's Animal Kingdom sometimes play matching games on computer tablets as a form of mental exercise.

The lights on the Christmas tree in front of Disney's Contemporary Resort are painted streetlamp bulbs that can be seen from 25 miles (40 km) away.

FOR HAUNTED MANSION HOLIDAY'S **20th** ANNIVERSARY AT DISNEYLAND, A ZOMBIE GINGERBREAD MAN'S EYES WERE IN THE SHAPE OF TWO ROMAN NUMERAL X'S.

THE LITTLE MERMAID (1989)
ANIMATORS STUDIED FOOTAGE
OF ASTRONAUT SALLY RIDE
FLOATING IN A SPACE
SHUTTLE TO CREATE
THE MOVEMENT OF
ARIEL'S HAIR UNDERWATER.

Lin-Manuel Miranda wrote *Encanto*'s (2021) "Waiting on a Miracle" in a **DIFFERENT BEAT** from the other songs in the movie to symbolize that Mirabel is an **outsider in her family.**

To research the **dancing animal** scenes in *Fantasia* (1940), one animator sat backstage at a ballet production for more than a week and drew **hundreds of sketches.**

SOME AUDIENCES SAW DIFFERENT VERSIONS OF THE ZNN NEWS ANCHOR IN ZOOTOPIA (2016): FANS IN CHINA WERE GREETED WITH A PANDA, AND THOSE IN AUSTRALIA, A KOALA.

Main Street Cinema in Disneyland once featured a costumed phantom that would frighten guests.

IN MONSTERS, INC. MIKE & SULLEY TO THE RESCUE! THERE ARE 236 DOORS IN THE DOOR VAULT SCENE.

A snow-simulation model used in the making of *Frozen* (2013) is helping scientists better understand avalanches.

Part of the inspiration for **WALL·E'S eyes** in *WALL·E* (2008) came from the movie's director playing with a pair of **binoculars at a baseball game.**

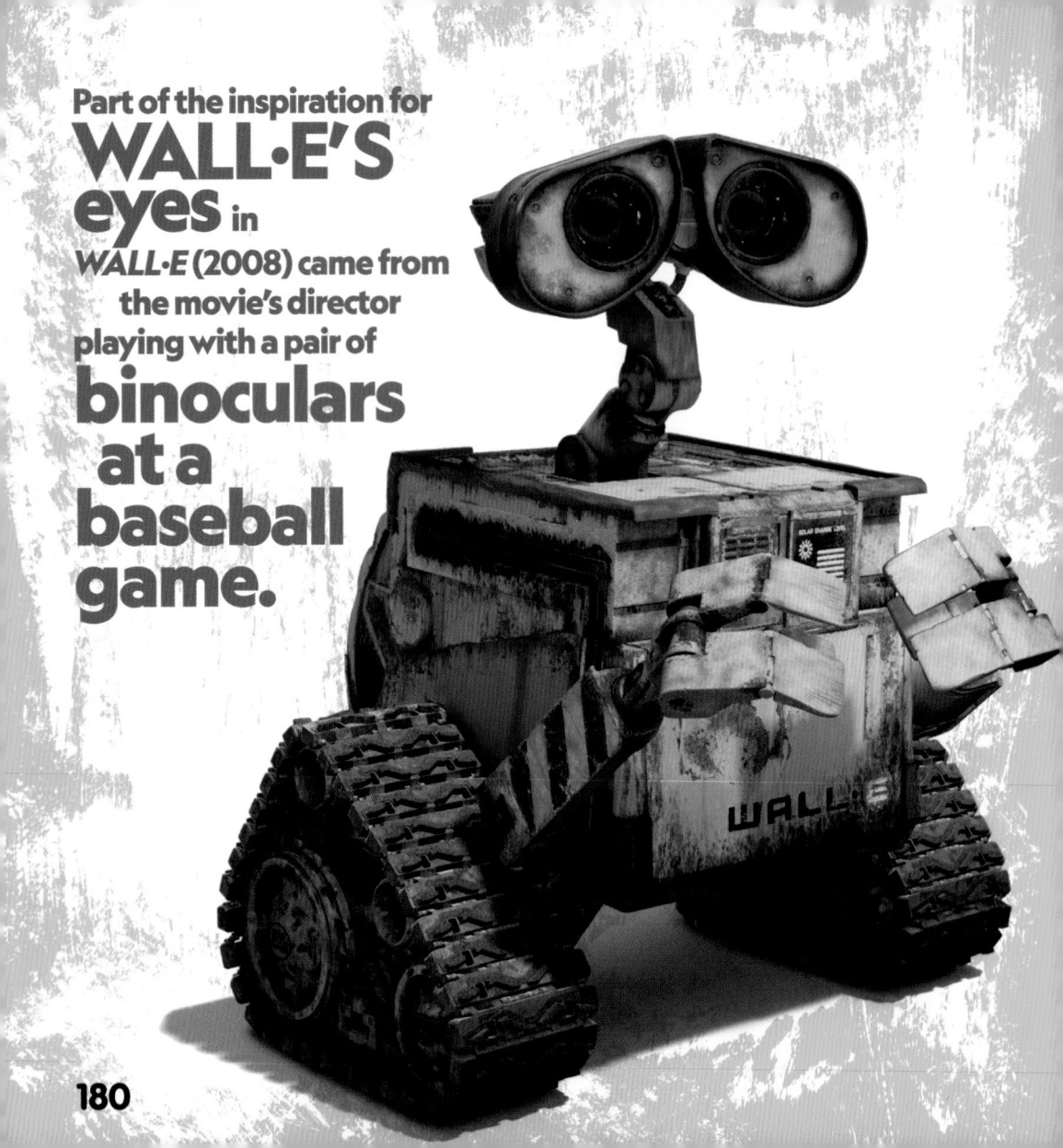

For a 2004 relay event honoring **Olympic swimmers,** Disneyland cast members **constructed a pool on Main Street, U.S.A.** in less than 30 hours.

TO ENSURE THAT A **RIDE ON SPACE MOUNTAIN** MIMICKED THE FEELING OF BEING IN SPACE, **NASA ASTRONAUT GORDON COOPER** HELPED IMAGINEERS DEVELOP THE COASTER'S CONCEPT.

LOCAL CHILDREN IN ITALY PROVIDED THE BACKGROUND KIDS' VOICES IN *LUCA* (2021).

THE ACTOR WHO VOICED ALBERTO RECORDED ALL HIS LINES IN HIS MOTHER'S CLOSET.

LUCA HAS 3,436 SCALES ON HIS SEA MONSTER BODY.

Pixar created a "bug cam" to help animators see the world from a bug's-eye view for *A Bug's Life* (1998).

ON A **SEVEN-NIGHT SAIL** ABOARD THE ***DISNEY MAGIC***, **7.5 TONS (6.8 T) OF CHICKEN, 7.5 TONS (6.8 T) OF MELON,** AND **71,500 EGGS** ARE EATEN, ON AVERAGE.

Guests eat an estimated 1.6 million corn dogs at Disneyland Resort each year.
Tivoli Gardens in Copenhagen, Denmark, one of the world's oldest amusement parks, was part of Walt Disney's inspiration for Disneyland.

PINOCCHIO (1940) ANIMATORS BUILT REAL MODELS OF SOME OF THE CLOCKS IN GEPPETTO'S WORKSHOP TO SHOW WALT DISNEY THAT THEY COULD ACTUALLY WORK.

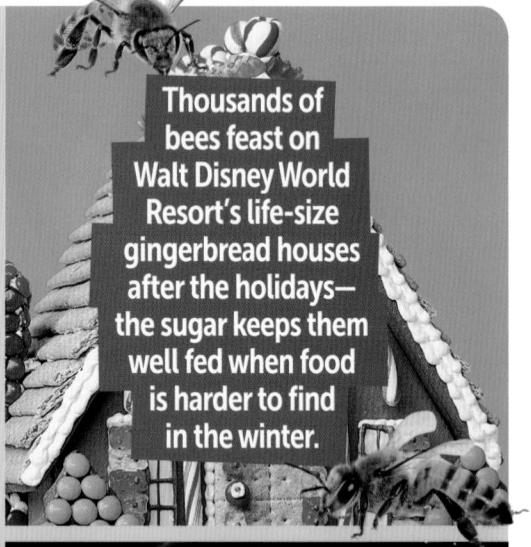

Thousands of bees feast on Walt Disney World Resort's life-size gingerbread houses after the holidays—the sugar keeps them well fed when food is harder to find in the winter.

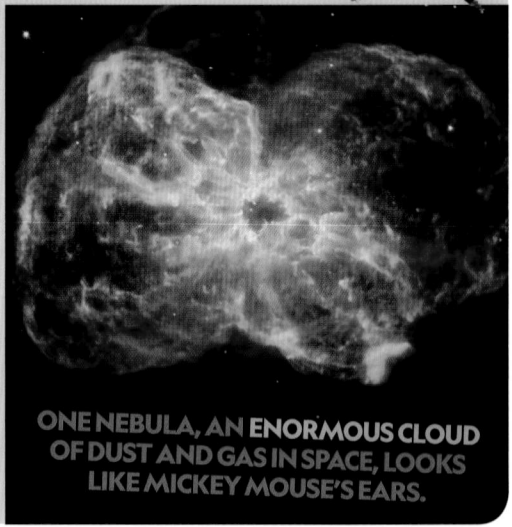

ONE NEBULA, AN ENORMOUS CLOUD OF DUST AND GAS IN SPACE, LOOKS LIKE MICKEY MOUSE'S EARS.

On the set of **Lady and the Tramp** (2019), the dog "stars" had their own trailer for hair and makeup, which included **fake dirt.**

IT TOOK MORE THAN **500,000 DRAWINGS** TO ANIMATE *ALICE IN WONDERLAND* (1951).

IN THE QUEUE FOR PETER PAN'S FLIGHT IN THE MAGIC KINGDOM, DECEMBER 27 IS CIRCLED ON THE CALENDAR IN THE NURSERY—THAT'S THE DATE J. M. BARRIE'S PLAY *PETER PAN* OPENED IN LONDON.

TONY'S TOWN SQUARE RESTAURANT AT THE MAGIC KINGDOM, NAMED FOR TONY FROM ***LADY AND THE TRAMP*** (1955), FEATURES **IMPRESSIONS OF THE PUPS' PAW PRINTS** IN THE PAVEMENT OUTSIDE.

WALT DISNEY WAS INSPIRED TO CREATE THE MATTERHORN BOBSLEDS ATTRACTION AFTER VISITING THE REAL-LIFE MOUNTAIN—HE SENT THE IMAGINEERS A POSTCARD OF THE PEAK THAT SAID

The horn signals for Disney Cruise Line ships play the first seven notes of "When You Wish Upon a Star."
RAPUNZEL AND FLYNN RIDER FROM *TANGLED* (2010) ATTEND ELSA'S CORONATION IN *FROZEN* (2013).

It took a year to make the **2.5-TON (2.3-T) STAINLESS STEEL PALM TREE** that lights the elephant exhibit for the sunset safari at Disney's Animal Kingdom.

YOU CAN FLOAT **400 FEET (122 M) HIGH** IN THE WORLD'S LARGEST **HAND-PAINTED** HELIUM BALLOON AT DISNEY SPRINGS.

Flamethrowers were used to create the **sound of the dragon's fiery breath** in *Sleeping Beauty* (1959).

Visitors to **TIFFINS RESTAURANT** in Disney's Animal Kingdom can see sketches that Imagineers made during their **around-the-world research trips** when planning the park.

Mickey & Minnie's Runaway Railway is the first Disney ride-through attraction to feature these characters.

The **unique orientation** of the desks in **Mei's classroom** in *Turning Red* (2022) is based on the director's **middle school experience.**

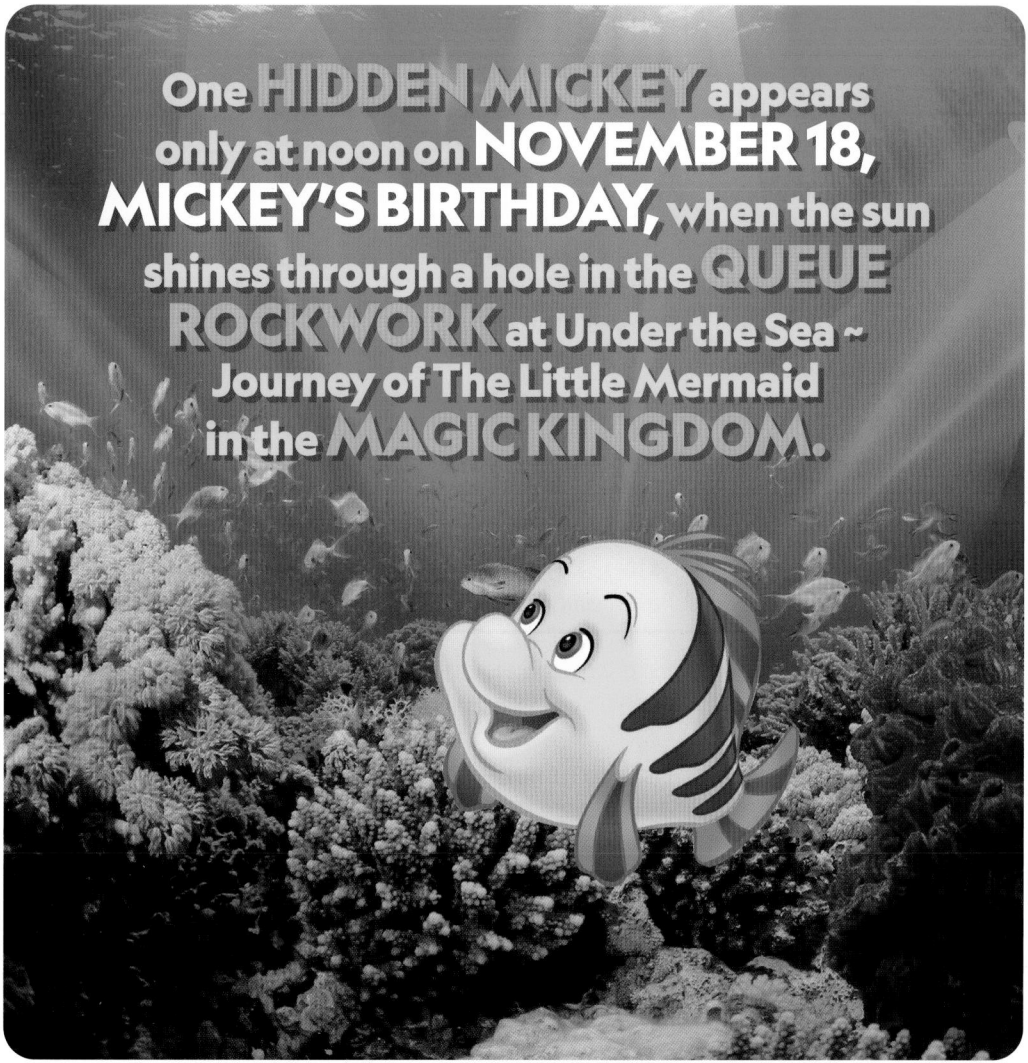
One HIDDEN MICKEY appears only at noon on NOVEMBER 18, MICKEY'S BIRTHDAY, when the sun shines through a hole in the QUEUE ROCKWORK at Under the Sea ~ Journey of The Little Mermaid in the MAGIC KINGDOM.

Boldface indicates illustrations.

A

Abu (*Aladdin* character) 100, **100**
Adélie penguins 156, **156–157**
Afar Depression, Africa 78, **78–79**
Aladdin (1992) 31, **31,** 100, **100**
Aladdin (Broadway) 80, 170
Alberto (*Luca* character) 182, **182**
Aldrin, Buzz 66, **66**
Alice in Wonderland (1951) 188, **188**
Angel Falls, Venezuela 147, **147**
Animal Kingdom *see* Disney's Animal Kingdom
Anton Ego (*Ratatouille* character) 66, **66**
AquaDuck **56–57,** 57
Ariel (*Little Mermaid* character) 97, 175
Arlo (*The Good Dinosaur* character) 135, **135**
Artemis Fowl (2020) 44, **44**
Astronauts 66, **66,** 175, **175,** 181, **181**
Astroturf 168, **168**
Audio-Animatronics® 67, 88, **88,** 96
Avalanches 179, **179**

B

Balloons **26–27,** 27, 104, 193, **193**
Barrie, J. M. 189
Baymax (*Big Hero 6* character) 119, **119**
Bears 46, **46,** 137, **137,** 151, **151**
Beast (*Beauty and the Beast* character) 46, **46,** 94, **138–139,** 139
Beauty and the Beast (1991) 46, **46,** 94, **94**
Beauty and the Beast (2017) **138–139,** 139
Belle (*Beauty and the Beast* character) 94, **94**
Big Hero 6 (2014) 119, **119**
Big Thunder Mountain Railroad 155, **155**
Bolt (2008) 81, **81**
Brave (2012) 128, **128**
A Bug's Life (1998) 184, **184**
Buzz Lightyear (Toy Story character) 66

C

California grizzly bears 137, **137**
Camels 195, **195**
Capuchin monkeys 100, **100–101**
Carl (*Up* character) 27
Cars (2006) 143, **143**
Centipedes 92, **92–93**
Chimpanzees 58–59, **58–59**
Cinderella (1950) 116, **116,** 171, **171**
Cinderella (2015) 158–159, **158–159**
Cinderella Castle 40, **40,** 44, **44,** 50–51, **50–51,** 160, **160**
Clinton, Bill 67, **67**
Coco (2017) 61, **61,** 127, **127**
Coney Island, New York, U.S.A. 141
Cooper, Gordon 181, **181**
Corey the Manticore (*Onward* character) 62, **62**
Corn dogs 185, **185**
Cucumbers 10, **10**

D

David Greybeard (chimpanzee) 58–59, **58–59**
Dean Hardscrabble (*Monsters University* character) 92, **93**
Descendants 2 (2017) 17
Dino-Sue 19, **19**
Disney, Walt
  arrival in Los Angeles 97
  birth date 168

childhood drawings 68, 112, **112**
Disneyland apartment 8, **8–9**
Disneyland inspiration 52, **52,** 185, **185, 190–191,** 191
in Disneyland lines 76
Disneyland's name 149
Disneyland's opening day 68
favorite animation 116, **116**
first named animated character **32–33,** 33
hometown 39, **39**
Jungle Cruise 140, **140**
love of trains 123, **123**
Mary Poppins penguins 163
Mickey Mouse's original name 28, **28**
as Mickey Mouse's voice 16, **16**
Pinocchio (1940) 186
"Storytellers" statue 117, **117**
Utilidor (tunnels) 36, **36**
Winnie the Pooh 91
Disney California Adventure
623 trolley 97, **97**
Grizzly Peak 137, **137**
The Little Mermaid ~ Ariel's Undersea Adventure 97, **97,** 160
Monsters, Inc. Mike & Sulley to the Rescue! 141, 179, **179**
morning power walk 131, **131**
Pixar Pal-A-Round 141, **141**
"Storytellers" statue 117, **117**
Toy Story Midway Mania! 96, 104
Disney Cruise Line
Christmas lights 134, **134**
food eaten 184
gingerbread cookies 124, **124**
horn signals 192, **192**
lifeboats 111, **111**
Pumpkin Trees 73
water coaster **56–57,** 57
Disney Dream (ship) **56–57,** 57
Disney Magic (ship) 184
Disney Springs 193, **193**
Disney World *see* Magic Kingdom; Walt Disney World Resort
Disneyland
40th anniversary time capsule 136, **136**
50th anniversary 65, **65**
entrance 99, **99**
Halloween celebration 74, **74**
Haunted Mansion Holiday 174, **174**
inspiration for 52, **52,** 185, **185, 190–191,** 191
"it's a small world" 136, 161
Jungle Cruise 10, **10,** 118, **118,** 140, **140**
King Arthur Carousel 102, **102**
Main Street, U.S.A. 39, **39,** 41, **41,** 90, **90,** 181, **181**
Main Street Cinema 179, **179**
Matterhorn 41, **41,** 134, 191
name 149
New Orleans Square 68
number of visitors 112, **112**
oldest object 73, **73**
opening day 68, 118
Peter Pan's Flight 28
Pirates of the Caribbean 28, 98, **98,** 104, **104,** 131
popcorn carts 109, **109**
Sleeping Beauty Castle 21, **21,** 53, **53,** 123, **123**
Town Square Fire Station 8, **8–9**
Walt Disney standing in line with guests 76
see also Haunted Mansion
Disneyland Paris **132–133,** 133, 134, 166, **166**
Disneyland Resort 141, 185, **185**
Disneynature films 151, **151,** 156, **156–157**

Disney's Animal Kingdom
Dino-Sue 19, **19**
DinoLand U.S.A. 88, **88**
elephants 34, **35,** 193, **193**
first animal born at 108, **108**
flamingos **152–153,** 153
food prepared each day **14–15,** 15
Forbidden Mountain 117, **117**
gibbons 173, **173**
gorilla's birthday cake 149
Himalaya mountains 63, **63**
hippos 152, **152**
"It's Tough to be a Bug!" 110
Kilimanjaro Safaris 44, **44,** 166, **166,** 172
lions 162, **162**
meerkats 152, **152**
Tiffins Restaurant 194, **194**
Tree of Life 45, **45, 58,** 58–59
Disney's Blizzard Beach Water Park 103, **103**
Disney's Contemporary Resort 48, **48,** 174, **174**
Disney's Hollywood Studios 12, **12,** 53, **53,** 54, **54,** 60, **60,** 137
Disney's Wilderness Lodge 89, **89**
Donald Duck 10, 49, **49,** 108, **108,** 118, **118**
Dubai Miracle Garden, United Arab Emirates 55, **55**
Dumbo (*Dumbo* character) 30, **30**
Dumbo octopuses 60, **60**
Dumbo the Flying Elephant (attraction) **4–5,** 5

E

Eiffel, Gustave 123
Elephants 34, **35,** 172, **172,** 193, **193**
Elsa (*Frozen* character) 150, **150,** 192
Encanto (2021) 42–43, **42–43,** 120, **120,** 176, **176**
EPCOT
Club Cool 99, **99**
France pavilion 117, 123
Guardians of the Galaxy: Cosmic Rewind 112, **112**
Italy pavilion 38, **38**
Land pavilion 10, 46, **46**
Mission: SPACE 47, **47,** 122, **122**
Planetary Plaza 47, **47**
The Seas with Nemo & Friends pavilion 148, **148**
Spaceship Earth 6, **6,** 47, **47**
Test Track 6, **6,** 20
World Showcase Lagoon 47, **47**
year opened 20
EPCOT International Flower & Garden Festival 121, **121**
Expedition Everest – Legend of the Forbidden Mountain 126, **126**

F

Fantasia (1940) 23, **23,** 177, **177**
Fantasmic! show 130, **130**
Fennec foxes 95, **95**
Finding Dory (2016) 168, **168**
Finding Nemo (2003) 48, **48,** 124, **124,** 127, **127**
Finnick (*Zootopia* character) 95, **95**
Fix-It Felix Jr. (video game) 168
Flamingos 22, **22, 152–153,** 153
Flynn Rider (*Tangled* character) 192, **192**
Frozen (2013) 150, **150,** 151, **151,** 179, **179,** 192, **192**

G

Geppetto (*Pinocchio* character) 186, **186**
Gibbons 173, **173**
Gino (gorilla) 149, **149**

Goats 77, **77**
The Good Dinosaur (2015) 135, **135,** 142, **142**
Goodall, Jane 59, **59**
Goofy 37, **37,** 68, **68**
Gorillas 46, **46,** 149, **149**
Grand Canyon, Arizona, U.S.A. 89, **89**
Guardians of the Galaxy: Cosmic Rewind 112, **112**

H

Halley's comet 122, **122**
Halloween 73, **73,** 74, **74,** 90, **90**
Hamsters 81
Hank (*Finding Dory* character) 168, **168**
Haunted Mansion
birthday candles 71, **71**
dancing ghosts 17, **17**
Hitchhiking Ghosts 154, **154**
names on tombstones 22, **22**
scary knight 70, **70**
singing busts 114–115, **114–115**
Haunted Mansion Holiday 174, **174**
Helicopters 53, **53**
Helium balloons 193, **193**
Hench (ride designer) 7
Hidden Mickeys 23, **23,** 137, 197, **197**
Hippos 152, **152, 177**
Hocus Pocus (1993) 167, **167**
Hollywood Studios *see* Disney's Hollywood Studios
Hollywood Walk of Fame 31, **31**
Hot-air balloons 193, **193**
Hôtel de Glace, Québec City, Canada 150
The Hunchback of Notre Dame (1996) 75

I

Imagineers 20, 22
"It's a small world" 99, 108, **108,** 136, 161
"It's Tough to be a Bug!" (3D film) 110

J

"Jolly Holiday" (song) 163, **163**
Julius the cat **32–33,** 33

K

Kevin (*Up* character) 125, **125**
Kudu 108, **108**

L

Lady and the Tramp (1955) 189, **189**
Lady and the Tramp (2019) 187, **187**
LEPrecon (*Artemis Fowl* characters) 44, **44**
Lesser flamingos **152–153,** 153
Liberty Bell 13, **13**
Lightyear (2022) 17
Lilo & Stitch (2002) 144–145, **144–145**
The Lion King (1994) 29, **29,** 85, **85,** 90
The Lion King (2019) 78, **78–79,** 162, **162**
The Lion King (Broadway) 80, 86
Lions 46, **46,** 162, **162**
The Little Mermaid (1989) 25, **25,** 97, 113, **113,** 175
The Little Mermaid ~ Ariel's Undersea Adventure 97, **97,** 160
Luca (2021) 182–183, **182–183**
Luca (*Luca* character) 183, **183**
Lucky (Audio-Animatronics® dinosaur) 88, **88**
Luigi (*Cars* character) 143
Lunar landings 47, 66, **66**

M

Mad Tea Party 5, **5**

The Magic Kingdom
Big Thunder Mountain Railroad 155, **155**
Cinderella Castle 40, **40,** 44, **44,** 50–51, **50–51,** 160, **160**
The Hall of Presidents 67
Liberty Square 11, **11,** 13, **13,** 160, **160**
The Magic Carpets of Aladdin 195, **195**
Main Street, U.S.A. 41, **41,** 122, 161, **161**
Peter Pan's Flight 189
Under the Sea ~ Journey of The Little Mermaid 197, **197**
Space Mountain 7, **7,** 181, **181**
Tony's Town Square Restaurant 189
Town Square Christmas tree 73, **73**
Utilidor (tunnels) 36, **36**
Walt Disney World Railroad 40, **40**
see also Haunted Mansion
Maleficent (2014) 62, **62**
Maleficent (*Sleeping Beauty* character) 77, **77**
Manatees 148, **148**
Map, Disney theme parks 64
Marceline, Missouri, U.S.A. 39, **39**
Mark Twain Riverboat 141, **141**
Mary Poppins (1964) 163, **163**
Mary Poppins (Broadway) 91
Matterhorn Bobsleds 191
Matterhorn mountain 41, **41,** 134, **190–191,** 191
Mayor Lionheart (*Zootopia* character) 90, **90**
Meerkats 152, **152**
Mei (*Turning Red* character) 196, **196**
Mercury (planet) 20, **20**
Merida (*Brave* character) 128, **128**
Mickey & Minnie's Runaway Railway 195, **195**
Mickey Mouse
actors voicing 16, **16,** 149, **149**
animators 126
birthday 105, 197
Disneyland Paris outfits **132–133,** 133
fan letters 87, **87**
first cartoon 54, 105, **105**
first words 22
floral sculptures 55, **55,** 99, **99**
Hidden Mickeys 23, **23,** 137, 197, **197**
memorabilia 98, **98**
Mickey & Minnie's Runaway Railway 195, **195**
name in other countries 124
original name 28, **28**
shoes 111, **111**
things shaped like his head 10, **10,** 20, **20,** 24, **24,** 98, **98,** 102, **102,** 186, **186**
Milne, A. A. 91
Mingsha Mountains, China 39, **39**
Minnie Mouse 105, 149, **149,** 195, **195**
Mirabel (*Encanto* character) 42, **42–43,** 120, **120,** 176, **176**
Miranda, Lin-Manuel 176
Moana (2016) 12, 34–35, **35,** 80, 87, **87**
Monkeys 100, **100–101,** 126
Monsters, Inc. (2001) 143, **143**
Monsters University (2013) 92, **93**
Monument Valley, Arizona and Utah, U.S.A. 155, **155**
Moon landings 47, 66, **66**
Mr. Potato Head (Toy Story character) 96
Mufasa (*Lion King* character) 90
Mulan (1998) 163
Mulan (2020) 39, **39**

N

Nautilus (*20,000 Leagues* ship) 169, **169**
Nebulae 186, **186**
Neuschwanstein Castle, Germany 53, **53**
Niagara Falls, Canada-U.S.A. 91, **91**
Notre Dame Cathedral, Paris, France 94, **94,** 166, **166**

O

Octopuses 60, **60,** 168, **168**
Olympic swimmers 181, **181**
One Hundred and One Dalmatians (1961) 10, **10,** 18, **18,** 36
Onward (2020) 62, **62,** 146, **146**

P

Penguins 119, **119,** 156, **156–157,** 163, **163**
Penguins (2019) 156, **156–157**
Peter Pan (1953) 172, **172, 189**
Peter Pan (play) 189
Peter Pan's Flight 28, 189
Pete's Dragon (1977) 77, **77**
Pinocchio (1940) 186, **186**
Pinocchio lizards 146, **146**
Pirates of the Caribbean (attraction) 28, 98, **98,** 104, **104,** 131
Pirates of the Caribbean: On Stranger Tides (2011) 96, **96**
Pizza Planet truck 129, **129**
Polar Bear (2022) 151, **151**
Prince Charming (*Cinderella* character) 171, **171**
The Princess and the Frog (2009) 81, **81**
Pumbaa (*Lion King* character) 86, **86**

R

Radiator Springs Racers 96, **96–97**
Rafiki (*Lion King* character) 85, **85**
Rapunzel (*Tangled* character) 12, **12,** 31, **31,** 192, **192**
Ratatouille (2007) 66, **66,** 84, **84,** 117, **117,** 126, **126**
Rattlesnakes **107**
Raya and the Last Dragon (2021) 13, **13**
Reindeer 151, **151**
Remy (*Ratatouille* character) 117, **117**
Renewable energy 24, **24**
Rhino (*Bolt* character) 81
Ride, Sally 175, **175**
Rock 'n' Roller Coaster Starring Aerosmith 12, **12,** 154
Rose, Anika Noni 81, **81**

S

Scarecrow (*Wizard of Oz* character) 72, **72**
Scents 28, 29
Sebastian (*Little Mermaid* character) 113, **113**
Secrets of the Whales (2021) **82–83,** 83
Sleeping Beauty (1959) 77, **77, 106–107,** 107, 123, 194, **194**
Sleeping Beauty Castle 21, **21,** 53, **53,** 123, **123,** 136, 166, **166**
Slinky Dog Dash 53, **53,** 60, **60**
Smithsonian Institution, Washington, D.C., U.S.A. 5
Snow White (Disney Princess) 31, **31**
Snow White and the Seven Dwarfs (1937) 105, **105**
Soarin' Around the World 29, **29,** 53, 134
Solar facilities 24, **24**
Soul (2020) 131, **131,** 142, **142**
Space Mountain 7, **7,** 181, **181**

Spaceship Earth 6, **6,** 47, **47**
Stained-glass windows 160, **160,** 166, **166**
"Steamboat Willie" (1928) 105, **105**
Stink bugs 110, **110**
"Storytellers" (statue) 117, **117**
Sulley (*Monsters, Inc.* character) 143, **143**
Summit Plummet waterslide 103, **103**
Sven (*Frozen* character) 151, **151**
Swiss Family Robinson (1960) 22, 168

T

T. rex 19, **19**
Tangled (2010) 12, **12,** 31, **31,** 192, **192**
Telegraph code 68, **68**
Tepuis 76, **76**
Terra-cotta warriors 163, **163**
Tiana (*Princess and the Frog* character) 81, **81**
Tinkerbella nana 172, **172**
Tivoli Gardens, Copenhagen, Denmark 185, **185**
Tokyo Disney Resort 102, **102**
Tony (*Lady and the Tramp* character) 189, **189**
Toy Story (1995) 66, 72, **72,** 76, **76,** 129
Toy Story 4 (2019) 84, **84**
Toy Story Land 53, **53**
Toy Story Midway Mania! 96, 104
Tree of Life 45, **45, 58,** 58–59
Tuk Tuk (*Raya* character) 13, **13**
Turning Red (2022) **164–165,** 165, 196, **196**
20,000 Leagues Under the Sea (1954) 48, 169, **169**
Tyrannosaurus rex 19, **19**

U

Under the Sea ~ Journey of The Little Mermaid 197, **197**
Up (2009) **26–27,** 27, 76, **76,** 125, **125,** 147, **147**
Utilidor 36, **36**

V

Volcanoes 38, **38**

W

"Waiting on a Miracle" (song) 176, **176**
WALL·E (2008) 91, 169, **169,** 180, **180**
Walt Disney World Resort 6, 21, **21,** 24, **24,** 50–51, **50–51,** 186, **186**; *see also* Magic Kingdom
Whales **82–83,** 83
"When You Wish Upon a Star" (song) 192
Winnie the Pooh 91, **91**
The Wise Little Hen" (1934) 72, **72,** 108, **108**
The Wizard of Oz (1939) 72, **72**
Woody (Toy Story character) 72, **72,** 84, **84**
Wreck-It Ralph (2012) 168, **168**

Y

Yen Sid (*Fantasia* character) 23, **23**

Z

Zootopia (2016) 90, **90,** 95, **95,** 178, **178**

PHOTO CREDITS

AD=Adobe Stock; AL=Alamy Stock Photo; DCP=Courtesy the Disney Consumer Products Creative Design team; DRMS=Dreamstime; GI=Getty Images; SS=Shutterstock; WDA=Courtesy of the Walt Disney Archives Photo Library; WDI=Walt Disney Imagineering

Cover, DCP; 1, DCP; 2, DCP; 3, DCP; 4-5, Molly Riley/Reuters; 5 (bursts), Kindlena/SS; 6 (UP), Michael Serraillier/Gamma-Rapho via GI; 6 (LO), solarseven/SS; 6 (wheels), Nykonchuk Oleksii/SS; 7 (UP), Ricardo Ramirez Buxeda/TNS via ZUMA Wire; 7 (LO), sripfoto/SS; 8-9 (all), WDA; 10 (LE), WDA; 10 (UP RT), Kent Phillips/Disney; 10 (LO RT), Peangdao/SS; 11, Sarah L. Gardner/NG Staff; 11 (flag), David Smart/SS; 12 (UP), Singleline/SS; 12 (lightning bolts), mhatzapa/SS; 12 (LO), Disney Enterprises/Photofest; 13 (UP LE), DCP; 13 (LO LE), Africa Studio/SS; 13 (RT), Edwin Verin/SS; 14-15 (background), Frederick Langrange/Disney; 14 (LE), Eric Isselée/AD; 14 (leaves), kvdkz/AD; 14 (RT), Olena/AD; 15, Richard Peterson/SS; 16 (UP LE), DCP; 16 (LO LE), rangizzz/SS; 16 (RT), WDA; 17 (UP LE & LO LE), KariHoglund/GI; 17 (UP CTR), Feng Yu/SS; 17 (UP RT), Li Ding/AD; 17 (LO RT), WDI Photography; 18, WDA; 19, Disney; 20, NASA/Johns Hopkins University Applied Physics Laboratory/Carnegie Institution of Washington; 21 (map), ink drop/AD; 21 (UP RT), Kent Phillips/Disney; 21 (LO), AaronP/Bauer-Griffin/GC Images/GI; 22 (UP LE), Coffeemill/SS; 22 (UP RT), Ilya Akinshin/SS; 22 (LO LE), Valentinar/DRMS; 22 (LO RT), Mikesilent/SS; 22 (stone), mrkevvzime/AD; 23 (UP LE), WDA; 23 (LO LE), peace_art/SS; 23 (UP CTR), Sarah L. Gardner/NG Staff; 23 (CTR LE), Preston Mack/Disney; 23 (CTR RT), Sarah L. Gardner/NG Staff; 23 (LO CTR), Sarah L. Gardner/NG Staff; 23 (LO RT), Sarah L. Gardner/NG Staff; 24 (UP), Soonthorn/AD; 24 (LO), Chloe Rice/Disney; 25, Everett Collection, Inc.; 26-27, Disney; 28 (LE), DCP; 28 (UP RT), Vibe Images/SS; 28 (hat), Kathrine Jensen/SS; 28 (LO RT), 32 pixels/AD; 29 (UP), StanislavBeloglazov/SS; 29 (LO), Walt Disney Pictures/Photofest; 30, RKO Radio Pictures/Photofest; 31 (LE), DCP; 31 (UP RT), Hayk_Shalunts/SS; 31 (LO RT), DCP; 32-33, WDA; 33 (UP), The Picture Art Collection/AL; 34-35 (stars), Allexxandar/SS; 34 (LO), Vector Tradition SM/SS; 35 (UP RT), DCP; 35 (LO), Kletr/AD; 36 (LE), Zadorozhnyi Vikto/SS; 36 (RT), DCP; 37, Art of Drawing/AL; 38, Wead/AD; 38 (pizza), Viktor/AD; 39 (UP), DCP; 39 (music), olegganko/SS; 39 (LO), MediaNews Group/Orange County Register via GI/Contributor; 40 (castle), Olga Thompson/Walt Disney World Resort via GI; 40 (scroll), Vadim Sadovski/SS; 40 (knight), topvectors/AD; 40 (LO), Douglas Carr/AL; 41 (LE), WDA; 41 (RT), Bob Desmond/Disney; 41 (hoop), sergiy1975/AD; 41 (ball), Africa Studio/SS; 42-43, DCP; 44 (UP LE), Gene Duncan/Disney; 44 (wind), John Takai/SS; 44 (RT), Eric Isselee/SS; 44 (LO LE), DCP; 45, VIAVAL/AL; 46 (UP), Walt Disney Pictures/Photofest; 46 (lion), Eric Isselee/SS; 46 (buffalo), Isselee/DRMS; 46 (boar), Eric Isselée/AD; 46 (gorilla), Eric Isselee/SS; 46 (wolf), Iakov Filimonov/SS; 46 (bear), vesta48/AD; 46 (LO), Pixel-Shot/AD; 47 (UP), Viavaltours/DRMS; 47 (clouds), Sealstep/SS; 47 (LO), WDI Photographer; 48 (LE), DCP; 48 (UP RT), WDA; 48 (LO RT), Disney; 49, WDA; 50-51, Disney; 52 (background), Nataliya Hora/DRMS; 52 (RT), Delphotostock/AD; 53 (LE), Boris Stroujko/SS; 53 (UP RT), WDI; 53 (LO RT), Nancy Nehring/GI; 54, jolly_photo/SS; 55, SMUKA/AL; 55 (LO LE), Itana/SS; 56-57, Kent Phillips/Disney; 58-59 (background), Natalia/AD; 58, Sarah L. Gardner/NG Staff; 59, CBS via GI; 60 (UP LE), Gerardo Mora/GI; 60 (UP CTR), Michael Thompson/DRMS; 60 (LO), NOAA Office of Ocean Exploration and Research, 2019 Southeastern U.S. Deep-sea Exploration; 61, DCP; 61 (UP LE), anaumenko/AD; 62 (grunge background), Miloje/SS; 62 (RT), DCP; 63, RSBPhoto1/AL; 63 (inset), Olga Danylenko/SS; 64, NG Maps; 65, Fred Prouser FP/Reuters; 65 (gold), Ron Dale/SS; 66 (UP), Lightfield Studios/AD; 66 (LO), DCP; 67, Ralph Alswang/William J. Clinton Presidential Library; 68 (confetti), Olga Rom/SS; 68 (candles), Srdjan Stefanovic/GI; 68 (LO LE), DCP; 68 (UP RT), onairjiw/AD; 68 (face), EkaterinaP/SS; 68 (LO RT), biancardi/SS; 69, WDA; 70, Vanessa Hunt/WDI; 71, Yuliia Davydenko/DRMS; 72 (LE), DCP; 72 (RT), MGM/Photofest; 73 (LE), Muzhik/SS; 73 (ornaments), graphixmania/SS; 73 (UP RT), Denis Belitsky/SS; 73 (pumpkin), topseller/SS; 73 (LO RT), Westhimal/DRMS; 74 (background), David Johnson/AD; 74 (bat), SP Vector Art/SS; 74 (tiger), apple2499/AD; 75, BigNazik/AD; 76 (LE), Disney; 76 (UP RT), dzmitry/AD; 76 (LO RT), paketesama/AD; 77 (LE), Trifonenko Ivan/AD; 77 (LO LE), WDA; 77 (RT), stokkete/AD; 77 (UP RT), WDA; 78-79, Lukas/AD; 78 (LO), WDA; 80 (LE), Inara Prusakova/SS; 80 (UP RT), LedyX/SS; 80 (LO RT), Ilya Akinshin/SS; 81 (UP), DCP; 81 (LO LE & LO RT), WDA; 82-83, Chris/AD; 84 (UP), DCP; 84 (LO), Mary Evans/Walt Disney Pictures/Pixar Animation Studios/Ronald Grant/Everett Collection, Inc.; 85, DCP; 86, DCP; 87 (UP), DCP; 87 (LO RT), Boris Rabtsevich/SS; 87 (Mickey), DCP; 88, WDI; 89 (LE), WDI; 89 (RT), Amineah/AD; 90 (UP), DCP; 90 (LO), Alexander Raths/AD; 91 (LE), DCP; 91 (UP RT), Chief Design/AD; 91 (LO RT), Silken Photography/SS; 92-93, DCP; 92, anatchant/AD; 93, DCP; 94, Mapics/AD; 94 (LO CTR), WDA; 95 (LE), Farinoza/AD; 95 (RT), DCP; 96 (LE), Prezoom/SS; 96 (UP RT), Antonio Gravante/SS; 96 (CTR RT), DCP; 97 (UP), Jess Allen/WDI; 97 (LO), WDI; 98 (LE), WDA; 98 (flames), rudvi/SS; 98 (UP RT), NYgraphic/SS; 98 (LO RT), DCP; 99 (UP LE), NG Maps; 99 (notes), Pavel K/SS; 99 (LO LE), Bob Desmond/Disney; 99 (bubbles), hiro.y/AD; 99 (LO RT), Pineapple studio/AD; 100-101, Petr Salinger/SS; 100, DCP; 102 (all), WDI; 103, Matt Stroshane/Disney; 104 (UP LE), Fer Gregory/SS; 104 (LO LE), concept w/SS; 104 (RT), pukach/SS; 104 (air), Tori Art/AD; 104 (popcorn), Ilya Akinshin/SS; 105 (UP), WDA; 105 (LO LE), Elena Schweitzer/SS; 105 (LO RT), WDA; 106-107, WDA; 107, Tom/AD; 108 (LE), DCP; 108 (UP RT), WDI; 108 (LO RT), EcoView/AD; 109, OLC Photographer/WDI; 109 (UP RT), Ilya Akinshin/SS; 110, Hway Kiong Lim/SS; 111, Darryl Brooks/DRMS; 111 (Mickey), DCP; 112 (UP LE), faraktinov/AD; 112 (LO LE), University of Southern California/Corbis Historical/GI; 112 (UP RT), Kent Phillips/Walt Disney World Resort; 112 (LO RT), Kenishirotie/AD; 113, DCP; 114-115, Katie Roser/WDI; 114 (notes), trinurul/AD; 116, WDA; 117 (LE), Mike Pucher/WDI; 117 (UP RT), DCP; 117 (LO RT), WDI; 118 (LE), zxczxc80/AD; 118 (confetti), pixelliebe/SS; 118 (TV), dreamerve/SS; 118 (static), Wakajawaka/SS; 118 (LO RT), vencav/AD; 118 (hat), DCP; 119 (LE), DCP; 119 (RT), Enrique/AD; 120, Walt Disney Studios Motion Pictures/Everett Collection, Inc.; 120 (UP LE), Milous Chab/DRMS; 121, Lucy Clark/AL; 122 (UP), bischy/GI; 122 (LO), Bernie Epstein/AL; 123 (UP LE), WDA; 123 (LO LE), Chloe Rice/Disney; 123 (RT), doomu/AD; 124 (LE), DCP; 124 (flags), twixx/AD; 124 (LO RT), Natalia Zakharova/DRMS; 125 (cassowary), Worakit Sirijinda/SS; 125 (ostrich), Gusak/AD; 125 (pheasant), RealityImages/AD; 125 (RT), DCP; 126 (LE), Danita Delimont/AD; 126 (UP RT), DCP; 126 (LO RT), NP27/SS; 127 (UP), DCP; 127 (LO), Courtesy Pixar; 127 (LO RT), Uros Petrovic/AD; 128, DCP; 129 (box), Mega Pixel/SS; 129 (slice), mhatzapa/SS; 130, Chloe Rice/Courtesy Disney; 131 (LE), NorthShoreSurfPhotos/AD; 131 (flag), Hugoht/DRMS; 131 (plate), Lonni/SS; 131 (UP RT), New Africa/AD; 131 (LO RT), amnaj/AD; 132-133, Laurent Viteur/GI; 133 (RT), DCP; 134 (LE), Kristyna Vagnerova/SS; 134 (bulb), crwpitman/SS; 134 (UP RT), kostikovanata/AD; 134 (LO RT), Tim UR/SS; 135, DCP; 136 (UP), Jess Allen/WDI; 136 (LO), Melica/SS; 137 (UP CTR), Disney; 137 (UP RT), Shino Iwamura/SS; 137 (LO), DCP; 138-139, Disney; 140, WDA; 141 (UP LE), Rasulov/SS; 141 (LO LE), Matthew Beard/Disney; 141 (UP RT), COLOA Studio/SS; 141 (LO RT), Jess Allen/WDI; 142 (UP), Walt Disney Studios Motion Pictures/Photofest; 142 (LO), DCP; 142 (gum), Madlen/SS; 143 (UP LE), NG Maps; 143 (UP CTR), Stuart Armstrong; 143 (license plate), TeddyandMia/AD; 143 (door), DCP; 143 (LO RT), DCP; 144-145, DCP; 144-145 (banner), Exposurestonature/DRMS; 146 (UP), DCP; 146 (LO), Richard/AD; 147, Alice Nerr/AD; 147 (CTR RT), Photofest/Buena Vista Pictures; 147 (clouds), Giraphics/SS; 148, Nicolas Larento/AD; 148 (CTR), gavran333/AD; 149 (UP LE), Srdjan Stefanovic/GI; 149 (LE), Courtesy Disney; 149 (UP RT), Stephen Shugerman/GI; 149 (LO RT), DCP; 150 (UP), DCP; 150 (snowflake), Kichigin/SS; 150 (LO), SerkanSenturk/AL; 151 (frost), XONOVETS/SS; 151 (UP LE), Dirk Van Geel/500px/GI; 151 (LO LE), DCP; 151 (UP RT), Timwege/DRMS; 151 (LO RT), Iakov Filimonov/SS; 152 (background), Maks Narodenko/AD; 152 (LE), Gubin Yury/SS; 152 (RT), Aaron Amat/SS; 153 (all), coffeemill/AD; 154 (UP), Kozlik/SS; 154 (LO), Andrea Barnett/Disney; 155, PolarPolar/SS; 155 (LO RT), Kent Phillips/Disney; 156-157, Ivan/AD; 158 (background), Morozova Oxana/SS; 158 (thread), Bunphot Kliaphuangphit/SS; 158 (silk), Khakimullin Aleksandr/SS; 158 (crystals), Julie Boro/AD; 159 (background), Coldmoon Photopro/SS; 159 (CTR), WDA; 160 (LE), WDI; 160 (UP RT), Sabina Schaaf/AD; 160 (brick), Dan Kosmayer/SS; 160 (LO RT), dule964/AD; 161, Andrea Barnett/Disney; 162, Jeff Nickel/Disney; 163 (UP), WDA; 163 (LO), Ratnakorn Piyasirisorost/GI; 164-165 (background), Creatus/AD; 164, Courtesy Pixar; 166 (LE), TAW4/AD; 166 (sticks), All For You/SS; 166 (RT), Isaac74/GI; 166 (CTR RT), Kent Phillips/Disney; 167 (background), Cattallina/AD; 167 (UP LE), Nathapol Kongseang/SS; 167 (UP RT), Mitch/AD; 167 (LO RT), serikbaib/AD; 168 (UP LE), DCP; 168 (CTR LE), anonpichit/AD; 168 (LO LE), iadams/AD; 168 (UP RT), Ilya Rumyantsev/AD; 168 (LO RT), gunungkawi/AD; 169 (UP), WDA; 169 (CTR LE), Steve Byland/DRMS; 169 (CTR RT), Paul Vinten/AD; 169 (LO), DCP; 170, SpicyTruffel/AD; 170 (CTR), Thomas/AD; 171, WDA; 172 (LE), DCP; 172 (CTR), Jennifer Read; 172 (RT), Talvi/SS; 173, Gerry Ellis/Photodisc; 173 (UP LE), 12bit/SS; 174 (UP), Disney; 174 (LO), Verock/SS; 175, NASA/JSC; 176, DCP; 176 (music), agrus/AD; 177, WDA; 178 (all), Courtesy Disney; 179 (UP LE), Kjpargeter/SS; 179 (LO LE), ProfiTrollka/AD; 179 (RT), Lysogor Roman/SS; 179 (UP RT), Comauthor/AD; 180, DCP; 181 (LE), nazarkru/AD; 181 (medal), aguiters/SS; 181 (UP CTR), NASA/JSC; 181 (RT), Disney; 182, DCP; 183, Courtesy Pixar; 184 (LE), Courtesy Pixar; 184 (UP RT), Superheang168/SS; 184 (LO RT), stable/SS; 185 (UP), michelaubryphoto/AD; 185 (LO), Jainhamer/DRMS; 186 (LE), WDA; 186 (UP RT), Courtesy of Solvang Bakery/Photography by Becky Hale/NG Staff; 186 (bees), vtupinamba/iStock Photo/GI; 186 (LO RT), NASA Goddard; 187, MediaPunch Inc/AL; 188, WDA; 188 (UP), warmworld/AD; 189 (LE), QQ7/AD; 189 (CTR LE), DCP; 189 (RT), donatas1205/SS; 189 (LO RT), DCP; 190-191, Jakl Lubos/SS; 192 (UP), albund/SS; 192 (stars), natakukushkina/AD; 192 (LO), Courtesy Pixar; 193 (LE), Twins Design Studio/AD; 193 (LO LE), Jakub Krechowicz/SS; 193 (RT), Supa Chan/SS; 193 (balloons), Kirill/AD; 194 (UP), WDA; 194 (CTR), Trybex/SS; 194 (LO), Mariah Wild/Courtesy Disney; 195 (UP RT), lovely pet/SS; 195 (spit), Olga Moonlight/SS; 195 (LO), Mike Pucher/WDI; 196, DCP; 196 (UP RT), AB Photography/AD; 197, Rich Carey/SS; 197 (lights), David Sandonato/DRMS; 197 (LO), DCP; 206, DCP

Copyright © 2023 Disney, All Rights Reserved,
Disney Entertainment, National Geographic.

All rights reserved. Reproduction of the whole or any part of the contents without written permission from the publisher is prohibited.

NATIONAL GEOGRAPHIC and Yellow Border Design are trademarks of the National Geographic Society, used under license.

Since 1888, the National Geographic Society has funded more than 14,000 research, conservation, education, and storytelling projects around the world. National Geographic Partners distributes a portion of the funds it receives from your purchase to National Geographic Society to support programs including the conservation of animals and their habitats. To learn more, visit natgeo.com/info.

For more information, visit nationalgeographic.com, call 1-877-873-6846, or write to the following address:

National Geographic Partners, LLC
1145 17th Street NW
Washington, DC 20036-4688 U.S.A.

For librarians and teachers: nationalgeographic.com/books/librarians-and-educators

More for kids from National Geographic: natgeokids.com

National Geographic Kids magazine inspires children to explore their world with fun yet educational articles on animals, science, nature, and more. Using fresh storytelling and amazing photography, *Nat Geo Kids* shows kids ages 6 to 14 the fascinating truth about the world—and why they should care. **natgeo.com/subscribe**

For rights or permissions inquiries, please contact National Geographic Books Subsidiary Rights: bookrights@natgeo.com

Designed by Eva Absher-Schantz

Trade paperback ISBN: 978-1-4263-7470-8
Reinforced library binding ISBN: 978-1-4263-7509-5

The publisher would like to thank the team that made this book possible: Grace Hill Smith, editor; Ariane Szu-Tu, editor; Sarah J. Mock, senior photo editor; Alix Inchausti, senior production editor; and Lauren Sciortino and David Marvin, associate designers.

Printed in Hong Kong
23/PPHK/1

The following are some of the trademarks, registered marks, and service marks owned by Disney Enterprises, Inc.: *Audio-Animatronics*® Figures; *Big Thunder Mountain*® Railroad; *Disney*®; *Disney California Adventure*® Park; *Disney Cruise Line*® Ships; *Disney Springs*™; *Disneyland*® Hotel; *Disneyland*® Park; *Disneyland*® Resort; *Disneyland*® Paris; *Disney's Animal Kingdom*® Theme Park; Disney's Contemporary Resort; *Disney's Hollywood Studios*®; Disney's Wilderness Lodge; *Downtown Disney*® Area; *Dumbo the Flying Elephant*® Attraction; *EPCOT*®; *EPCOT International Flower & Garden Festival*; *Fantasyland*® Area; *Frontierland*® Area; *Hong Kong Disneyland*® Resort; Imagineering; Imagineers; "it's a small world"; *It's a Small World*® Attraction; *Magic Kingdom*® Park; *Main Street, U.S.A.*® Area; monorail; *Shanghai Disneyland*® Park; *Shanghai Disney*® Resort; *Space Mountain*® Attraction; *Tokyo Disney*® Resort; *Tokyo Disneyland*® Park; *Tomorrowland*® Area; *Walt Disney World*® Resort; and World Showcase.

The following attractions, films, and all associated characters are © Disney: *Aladdin*; *Alice in Wonderland*; *Beauty and the Beast*; *Bolt*; Captain Nemo; *Cinderella*; *Descendants 2*; Dippy Dawg; Donald Duck; *Dumbo*; *Fantasia*; *Frozen*; Goofy; Haunted Mansion Holiday; *Hocus Pocus*; Julius the Cat; *Lady and the Tramp*; *Lilo & Stitch*; *Maleficent*; *Mary Poppins*; Mickey Mouse; Minnie Mouse; *Moana*; *Mulan*; *Pete's Dragon*; *Pinocchio*; *Raya and the Last Dragon*; *Sleeping Beauty*; "Steamboat Willie"; *Tangled*; "The Karnival Kid"; *The Lion King*; *The Little Mermaid*; *The Princess and the Frog*; *Wreck-It Ralph*.

The following live theater productions are © Disney, All Rights Reserved: *Aladdin*; *Mary Poppins*; *The Lion King*.

The following characters, films, and productions are © Disney/Pixar: *A Bug's Life*; *Brave*; *Cars*; *Coco*; *Encanto*, *Finding Dory*; *Finding Nemo*; "It's Tough to be a Bug!"; *Lightyear*; *Luca*; *Monsters, Inc.*; Monsters, Inc. Mike & Sulley to the Rescue!; *Monsters University*; *Onward*; Pixar Pal-A-Round; *Ratatouille*; *Soul*; *The Good Dinosaur*; Toy Story (all); *Turning Red*; *WALL·E*; *Up*; *Zootopia*.

20,000 Leagues Under the Sea © Disney. Based on the work *20,000 Leagues Under the Sea* by Jules Verne.

Artemis Fowl © Disney. Based on the work *Artemis Fowl* by Eoin Colfer.

Big Hero 6 © Disney. Based on the work "Big Hero 6" by Man of Action.

Club Cool Hosted by Coca-Cola.

Disney's Solar Facilities are operated by Duke Energy, North Carolina.

Guardians of the Galaxy: Cosmic Rewind © Disney Enterprises, Inc./Marvel.

The Hunchback of Notre Dame © Disney. Based on the work *The Hunchback of Notre-Dame* by Victor Hugo.

LEGO, the LEGO logo, the Brick and Knob configurations are trademarks of the LEGO Group. © 2023 The LEGO Group. All rights reserved.

The Little Mermaid © Disney. Based on the work "The Little Mermaid" by Hans Christian Andersen.

Mr. Potato Head® is a registered trademark of Hasbro, Inc. Used with permission. © Hasbro, Inc.

One Hundred and One Dalmatians © Disney. Based on the book *The Hundred and One Dalmatians* by Dodie Smith published by The Viking Press.

Penguins © Disneynature.

Peter Pan © Disney. Based on the Peter Pan works by J. M. Barrie.

Pinocchio © Disney. Based on the work *The Adventures of Pinocchio* by Carlo Collodi.

Pirates of the Caribbean: On Stranger Tides © Disney Enterprises, Inc. Based on characters created by Ted Elliott & Terry Rossio and Stuart Beattie and Jay Wolpert. Based on Walt Disney's Pirates of the Caribbean. Suggested by the novel by Tim Powers. Screen Story and Screenplay by Ted Elliott & Terry Rossio.

Pixar properties © Disney/Pixar.

Polar Bear © 2022 Disney Enterprises, Inc. All Rights Reserved.

The Seas with Nemo & Friends © Disney/Pixar, The Seas with Nemo & Friends Attraction inspired by the Disney and Pixar film *Finding Nemo*.

Secrets of the Whales © Disney, All Rights Reserved, Disney Entertainment, National Geographic.

Slinky Dog © POOF-Slinky, LLC; © Slinky, © Dog, © Just Play.

Snow White and the Seven Dwarfs © Disney. Based on the work "Snow White" by the brothers Grimm.

Swiss Family Robinson © Disney. Based on the work *The Swiss Family Robinson* by Johann David Wyss.

Winnie the Pooh characters based on the "Winnie the Pooh" works by A. A. Milne and E. H. Shepard.

"The Wise Little Hen" © Disney. Based on the fable "The Little Red Hen."

AMP UP YOUR NERD CRED

From **SUPERHEROES** to **UFOs** and **VIKINGS** to **EDIBLE BUGS,** here's everything a **NERD** could want to know.

NATIONAL GEOGRAPHIC KIDS

AVAILABLE WHEREVER BOOKS ARE SOLD

Discover more at natgeokids.com

© 2023 National Geographic Partners, LLC